THE
REFORMATION IN
ENGLAND

BY
SIR MAURICE POWICKE

*Sometime Regius Professor of Modern History
in the University of Oxford*

OXFOR.   ᴿᴱSS

Oxford University Press, Amen House, London E.C.4

GLASGOW NEW YORK TORONTO MELBOURNE WELLINGTON
BOMBAY CALCUTTA MADRAS KARACHI KUALA LUMPUR
CAPE TOWN IBADAN NAIROBI ACCRA

First edition 1941
Reprinted 1942, 1949, 1953 and 1958
First issued in OXFORD PAPERBACKS 1961

Printed in Great Britain by Richard Clay and Company, Ltd.,
Bungay, Suffolk

CONTENTS

THE REFORMATION IN ENGLAND

I. THE MEDIEVAL BACKGROUND OF THE REFORMATION IN ENGLAND

THE one definite thing which can be said about the Reformation in England is that it was an act of State. The King became the head of the Church, the King in Parliament gave a sanction to the revised organization, formularies, liturgy, and even in some degree to the doctrine of the Church. The King's Council and Ministers took cognizance of ecclesiastical affairs. The King co-operated with the bishops and convocation in the government of the Church, and he appointed commissions to determine appeals in ecclesiastical cases. All this amounted to a revolution. In earlier times there had, of course, been constant co-operation between secular and ecclesiastical authorities in matters ecclesiastical. Movements of thought tending to the isolation of the two authorities from each other had not been successful in the Middle Ages. Although there was much difference of opinion about the origin and rights of secular authority, some saying that it had a divine sanction as part of the nature of things, others contending that after the coming of Christ it was derived from the successors of Christ, that is from the Church, and in particular from the Pope, very few were prepared to deprecate it, to regard it as a necessary evil. Indeed, in the best thought, human society was one, held together and inspired by belief in and obedience to God in a visible Church which comprised all Christian people, but also directed in this life by various kinds of secular authority. As is well known, idealists still believed in the necessity, if not in the actual existence, of a single secular ruler, to whom other rulers could look as subordinate authorities looked to them; but this theory was going out of fashion before the Reformation. In actual fact secular authority was bound up with the traditions of the group or community in which it resided; it could be regarded as democratic in its origin, although its justification depended upon its harmonious reaction to the moral law. But it was not sufficient in or for itself. It could not claim to lead its fraction of the whole Christian society in all the social activities of this life. It was so important that its co-operation was desired, it might be so powerful that the limits which it imposed upon the activities of the ecclesiastical authorities—who were linked together under the Pope in the government of the whole society—might have to be treated with acquiescence or even made the matter of formal agreement, but, strictly speaking, such limitations were forms of usurpation. For example, it was not unfitting that a King should have some voice in the election of a bishop; society was so intricate, secular and ecclesiastical functions so bound up together, that the royal licence to elect a bishop must be requested and given, and it was more than discourteous to elect a man who was not likely to be useful or was known to be distasteful to the King; or, again, friendly joint pressure on the part of King and Pope in favour of a particular candidate or a combined nomination actually overriding the electing body, might be advisable. But brutal insistence that such and such a man must be elected was a gross interference with canonical order. It would be hard to say, here and in many other ways, where agreement ended and usurpation began. The tactful exercise of Papal authority, by the use of dispensations or of the Papal 'plenitude of power', was required all the time in the later Middle Ages to oil the wheels. Yet that, ecclesiastically, society was one, greater than any political divisions, was a fundamental doctrine; nay, it was regarded as a natural fact. Hence the action of Henry VIII and his successors amounted to a revolution.

It is hard to resist the conclusion that the ease with which this revolution was effected was due to the prevalent system of compromise and not to any widespread belief in the necessity of change. As we shall see later, the momentous step was so easy that its significance was not faced. Facts, as usually happens, were more potent than theory, and when the time came for elaborate explanation, it was maintained that, as a matter of historic fact, the development of a united Christendom under Papal guidance had itself involved a gross usurpation of the rights of bodies politic, and that Christian unity was not bound up with the supremacy of Rome. Indeed, so it was claimed, the usurpation of the Pope was such a monstrous perversion of the true nature of the Church as to stamp him as Antichrist. At first this re-reading of history was confined to a very few. Henry VIII and his Parliament were content with the statement, surprising enough to us, but a very significant description of policy, that 'by divers sundry old authentic histories and chronicles it is manifestly declared and expressed that this realm of England is an Empire . . . governed by one supreme head and king . . . unto whom a body politic, compact of all sorts and degrees of people, divided in terms and by names of spiritualty and temporalty, be bounden and ought to bear, next to God, a natural and humble obedience'. In any 'cause of the law divine', it was within the power of the spiritualty 'now being usually called the English Church' to declare and determine 'without the intermeddling of any exterior person or persons'.[1] To maintain the independence of England as against any foreign interference was the first concern. Hence in 1534 a definite 'conclusion' was proposed in accordance with royal mandate to the convocations of Canterbury and York and to the Universities of Oxford and Cambridge; it was in the simple form 'Whether the Roman Pontiff has any great jurisdiction bestowed on him by God in the Holy Scriptures in this realm of England than any other foreign bishop?' There were four votes in favour of papal jurisdiction in the

[1] Act in restraint of appeals, 1533, 24 Hen. VIII, c. 12.

convocation of Canterbury, none in that of York. But the problems which are raised by the attempt to observe the 'law divine' in an independent state, and still more by the attempt to base national policy on the teaching of Holy Scripture, were not faced at this stage. Yet they are the fundamental issues in the development of the Reformation.

The cause of a united Christendom was not left without witness; yet it is to be observed that, with two great exceptions, only two or three cartloads of monks were willing to die for it. One of these monks, Dr. Richard Reynolds of Sion Monastery, had some reason for asserting that at heart the greater part of the kingdom was of their opinion, but opinion was not deep-rooted and was easily stifled by fear and bewilderment. Even the friars, the old militia of the church, were divided, and the practical opposition of a few was soon checked. The Carthusians, most remote from the world and also the least numerous in England of monks of the great medieval orders, were the most determined in opposition. The two great exceptions to the acquiescence of the laity and clergy were Bishop Fisher of Rochester and Sir Thomas More. After sentence had been passed upon him, More, for the first time, gave free expression to his views. No temporal lord could be head of the spiritualty; just as a child cannot refuse obedience to his natural father, so the realm of England could not refuse obedience to the see of Rome. His isolation signified nothing: for every bishop opposed to him, he could call upon a hundred saints, against every parliament he could appeal to the general councils of a thousand years:

You have no authority, without the consent of Christendom, to make a law or act of Parliament contrary to the common body of Christendom.

This was the witness of a man who had brooded long over the state of Christendom. He was wise, witty, urbane; observant, critical, caustic, yet full of pity. In his inner life he was austere, and could withdraw himself easily from the society in which he always shone, with a charm that captivated kings and bishops, nobles and all scholars, and brought him near to the common man. He found every place home in which he could be near to God. He believed as easily and intimately in the communion of saints as the ordinary citizen believed in the reality of the passer-by who jostled him in the street. Erasmus says of him that he talked with his friends about the future life as one speaking from the heart, with full hope; and it has been observed that what seemed to him 'the most terrible thing in the clamour for the plunder of church endowments was that it involved, not only social injustice, but the cessation of prayer for the dead': in his own words, 'that any Christian man could, for very pity, have founden in his heart to seek and study the means, whereby a Christian man should think it labour lost, to pray for all Christian souls'. The two cardinal tenets in the religion of Utopia are the belief in Divine Providence and in immortality.[1] Such was More in his inner life. But he was also a public man, shrewd and clear-sighted, compact of observation and pity. He had no illusions about the state of Europe. He was not a fanatical churchman, nor a thorough-going papalist. Indeed it would appear that at one time he was ready to welcome a general council which might even depose the Pope. He was a leader in the new learning and interested in the discovery and exploitation of the empty spaces of the earth. What he could not stand was the denial of the unity of Christendom, and that men should take advantage of the troubles of the time to decry this unity for the sake of power or money. He could see no rhyme or reason in the incessant wars, no justice in movements which spoiled the poor, no wisdom in the destruc-

---

[1] R. W. Chambers, *The Saga and the Myth of Sir Thomas More*, 1926 (Proceedings of the British Academy). Those who have read this fine essay—with the historical background of which I do not altogether agree—will see how much I am indebted to it.

tion of great institutions and ancient loyalties because they were not all that they should be. Hence, while nobody was more conscious than he of the impossibility, if not the folly, of trying to restrain the individual conscience, he was indignant against all disturbers of the peace in matters of opinion. There he was least in line with the new point of view. The state of things was so precarious, so many people were so headstrong, vain, ignorant, and irresponsible, fostering schisms which they could not control. In his public capacity he would naturally be expected to issue, and did issue, certificates which would give effect to the ecclesiastical law against heretics; although it is untrue that he actively set the law in motion—which was not his business—and insulted or persecuted heretics, he would see no inconsistency with his general outlook on life in the attempt to suppress the spread of Lutheran doctrines, especially if they were expressed with clamour or ostentation. With the perplexed, on the other hand, he was patient and persuasive; his own son-in-law was for a time, while a member of his household, attracted by the new views. Similarly, he took no public part in opposition to the royal policy and its developments. He refused to take the Oath of Supremacy, and rather than take it he died, but he would not have raised his voice if he had not been faced with the necessity of decision. Only if we had been in his position could we tell if his conduct was too cautious. whether he delayed unduly in putting his principles of order and loyalty before his duty to God. In his *Utopia* he had conveyed his deepest convictions in the fanciful form congenial to a child of the new learning. He was one of the first men to introduce the spirit of Plato into political discussion, but it never could have occurred to him, any more than it occurred to the long line of Platonic divines in the later Anglican Church, that his loyalty to the Church could be questioned. His Utopian people were dressed in Franciscan garb. They worshipped in the dark, mysterious, sumptuous churches which he loved. They recog-

nized in European monasticism an institute with which
they could sympathize. They would have nothing to do
with violence and intransigence of thought. It is possible
to push the analogy between the society of Utopia and the
society of united Christendom too far, but the two societies
are not inconsistent in principle. More wished to see, as so
many idealists in the Middle Ages had wished to see, a
really united and peaceful Christendom, striving ener-
getically to prepare itself for the life with God, despising
and rejecting capitalistic divisions in society, confident in
the fundamental harmony of reason and beauty and law
with the experience of the Church. Such faith in the possibilities of the future may well astonish us. For all his wit and
shrewdness, Sir Thomas More was a dreamer, not reckon-
ing enough with the untidy, disrespectful adventurousness
in the spirit of man. He had no experience of the explosive
power of conviction, whether it is right or wrong. But he
stands out as the one person who saw quite clearly what
Henry VIII's revolution meant; and, in the contrast between him and the people about him, we can see how far
religious society had drifted in the current of secularism
and compromise from the acceptance of the medieval
system, however irksome or imperfect, as beyond question.
Other interests and loyalties were now so natural, so much
a matter of course, that, if need be, the old could go. The
thoughtless could safely feel indifferent to them, not caring
much what came to take their place. More's wife, Mistress
Alice, could not understand why, for the sake of an oath,
Master More should suffer himself to lie in a close filthy
prison, shut up amongst mice and rats.

'Is not this house,' quoth he, 'as nigh heaven as mine own?'
To whom she, after her accustomed homely fashion, not liking
such talk, answered 'Tilly vally, Tilly vally.'

In the course of the century men gradually entered
upon a view of life, or rather upon several views of life,
very different from that of Sir Thomas More, though

equally important in their eyes, and maintained with conviction and passion. Doubtless a few saw their way clearly, even in the early days of change. There had been little groups of men who at the universities had been inspired by the teaching of Luther. In various parts of England, for example in the Chiltern Hills and the Forest of Dean, were families which held Lollard views as part of their inheritance. The scepticism which frequently went with the new learning had in some minds, especially the minds of courtiers and men of affairs, given a sharper edge to religious indifference. But Sir Thomas More was undoubtedly right in thinking that he was faced by men who, for the most part, did not know and did not seem to care where they were going. The more light is thrown upon the feelings of men at this time, even of the inmates of monasteries, the clearer this incapacity for sustained conviction seems to be. There was widespread indignation against the King's treatment of Queen Catherine; the royal insistence that More and Fisher should declare themselves was probably due to the fear that, if criticism and passive resistance were not quelled in high quarters, the management of the public temper might become too difficult; yet the general acquiescence is one of the most mysterious things in our history, and remains, from the point of view of the historian, the chief explanation of the drastic treatment of the Church and the ruthless spoliation of the religious houses.

Our difficulty in comprehending the course of events is doubtless partly due to the fact that to the modern mind English history does seem to begin again with the Reformation. We can see the results of the revolution and we tend to suppose that they were equally obvious at the beginning of the sixteenth century. Our categories are more clearly defined, and as we find it hard to think of England as other than a Protestant country, so we are disposed to feel, if not to think, that the Reformation was, as it were, a rebound to the normal, and the more self-conscious because it appears to have been so easy. This attitude is nothing more than a form of our insular self-possession, and the ease with which King Henry made himself supreme was due to a situation precisely the opposite of that which we imagine. Ecclesiastical opinion had become distracted by a long indulgence in compromise. The work of the Church had been done under the direction, first of great missionaries and bishops, then of great popes supported by men who were ready to suffer in the cause of unity, because they saw that only through unity could the work of the Church be done. In the course of this work, the organization of the Church had been perfected under Papal leadership. Probably the last really big Englishman to see clearly what this achievement involved was Robert Grosseteste, the bishop of Lincoln, who died in 1253. He saw, as he felt, with all the energy of his being. He was puzzled and distressed to find that what was so clear to him was so hard for others. In his eyes rights and duties were but different sides of the same thing, easily to be understood in the light of Scripture, the revelation of that law of nature of which they were expressions. It might be necessary to disobey the Pope and to suffer the consequences, but to disobey the Pope in the interests of man was unthinkable. The Church had in its keeping the moral and spiritual welfare of its children; it had contrived a system of law and administration which, within its own sphere, was supreme; it could not, without treachery to God and dishonour to itself, acquiesce in any interference with its courts by the secular power. The secular power, though inferior in status, had been devised to co-operate with the ecclesiastical in one great society; it had its own duties, rights, and functions, subject to the law of God, and within its scope all honour and obedience were due to it. But in a case of conflict, whether in jurisdiction or policy, the ministers of God, and particularly the bishops, could not hesitate about the course they should take. They should keep themselves at liberty, and, in accordance with the canons, refuse to

involve themselves in secular business. It was not for them
to sit in secular courts as judges; they had their own
duties, already hard enough, and if they did their work
properly, even too much for them. So Grosseteste taught.
Yet, as one reads his correspondence, one sees that the
effort to maintain the ecclesiastical system without compromise was hopeless. To his colleagues, able and practical
men as most of them were, this rigidity was tiresome. Why
stress these dilemmas in a world already difficult enough?
Here are two great powers for good, working together in
God's service. Why should a bishop not act as a secular
judge? Why should he, and the Pope too, not do a good
turn to a royal servant who deserved well of the King and
was in need of a benefice? If, in all kinds of ways, the law
which was being defined in the royal courts was inconsistent with the Canon Law administered in the
ecclesiastical courts, why not come to some working agreement, so that squabbles about advowsons, and tithes and
legitimacy and wills and all the rest of it may cease? There
was no question of heresy; England was quite free from
the dangerous unrest which prevailed from time to time in
the Rhineland and north Italy, in Champagne, and the
south of France. If English ecclesiastics were too logical
and stiff-necked, they would provoke in court-circles and
among their lay patrons a persistent anti-clericalism and
be forced into much closer subservience to the Papal court
than was pleasant. For if, on the one hand, they had to face
at home the constant intervention of the King and his
judges in ecclesiastical administration, they were, on the
other hand, increasingly at the mercy of Papal demands
for taxes and benefices. Hence the English clergy, who had
a strong national sense, tended to acquiesce in a middle
course. And, for the sake of peace, King and Pope tended
in the same direction.

    It is this tendency to compromise which has caused so
much misunderstanding and perplexity to historians of
the medieval Church in England. Every one has been able

to find, or to imagine that he had found, what he set out to find. The Puritan lawyers of the seventeenth century, led by the learned William Prynne, thought that they could trace in the Middle Ages the gradual vindication of the royal supremacy, or rather of the secular law, over the law and administration of the Church. The high church-man of a later day has often thought that he could estab-lish the existence of an independent *ecclesia Anglicana*, whose system of law, while influenced by that of the uni-versal Church, had its own sanctions. Both saw in the exercise of Papal control a kind of usurpation. They neglected or were unaware of the variety of local custom which was permitted to survive in various parts of the Church, and also of the element of compromise which existed in one form or another in every country, as well as in insular England, without prejudice to the belief in the essential unity of the Church. Today it is hardly necessary to point out that compromise was practical and oppor-tunist rather than a matter of principle. It was liable to interruption by the reassertion of principle at any time. It was like an uneasy truce between jurisdictions each of which claimed control over a strip of border territory, and it would have been unmeaning if the validity of each juris-diction within its own domain had not been generally recognized. Yet the fact that both Puritan lawyers and high churchmen could see what they saw in medieval England is very significant. Their interpretations do reflect, with some distortion, the peculiarities of English ecclesiastical life after it ceased to be controlled by men like Grosseteste.

An adequate analysis of these peculiarities would re-quire a discussion of English society as a legal and political organization. Here we must be brief. The main thing to be noted is the importance of the common law as an expression of the unity of England. In the later Middle Ages there was no State within the State. The laity in England, and also in other countries, had a parochial life and definite duties and responsibilities, social and moral, as members of the

Church of Christ, but they had no part in ecclesiastical organization. They were not faced by the dilemma of a decision between two forms of citizenship for the simple reason that the political organization was regarded as Christian, protecting the spiritual interests, not in opposition to them. If, for example, a man refused to accept the decision of an ecclesiastical court against him, he would be forced to obey by the secular power. In England the secular power was very penetrating. There were no ecclesiastical princes in England, no areas, with the exception (and from this point of view it was not a real exception) of the bishopric of Durham, in which a bishop or abbot was supreme; for the immunities of a great ecclesiastic were not marks of sovereignty, but of delegated royal power. Within his 'liberty', if he had one, he exercised the functions of sheriff or bailiff of the hundred, or, to put the matter more precisely, his officials took the place of royal officials and he received certain dues which were normally paid into the royal exchequer. He lived under the direction of the royal courts, within the sphere of the common law. Moreover he might be involved in secular duties, like any other citizen, as a minister of state, a royal commissioner, a member of the Great Council or House of Lords. His local prestige did not help him when he sat in the convocation of the clergy. Hence, although we hear a great deal about the *ecclesia Anglicana* we can trace no tradition in England of an organized body or church with an independent claim or status. As Maitland pointed out, the conciliar movement passed almost unnoticed in England. At one time there had been a possibility of a locally organized Christendom, in which the English convocation with its representative system of the clergy might have played a part, but in the fifteenth century we find nothing which corresponds in England to that movement in France which later, in co-operation with the Crown, was to shape the system of 'Gallican liberties'. Many of the clergy, many old established institutions like the Benedictine monastery of St. Albans, doubtless felt as definitely as the laymen that they belonged to England rather than to Rome. They were Englishmen, with an Englishman's dislike of the foreigner. They hated Papal taxation and Papal interference with the rights of patronage. They acquiesced cheerfully in the limitations imposed by the common law upon the operations of the ecclesiastical courts, just as they expected to be protected in their exemptions and privileges as clerics. In the ordinary life of every day they felt no incoherence, no difficulty; but this was because they were English, not because they had worked out any theory of a separate English Church. And in the same way they accepted the church order of a united Christendom under a Pope because it was the only conceivable order, and because they had no more inclination to heresy than they had to treason. The common law of England and the King accepted it all, with one all-important proviso. The King and the Pope worked together. The Papal powers, as they grew, were at the King's service for the reward of his friends and servants. The whole system of Papal taxation, so laboriously developed in defence of the Holy Land, was gradually changed into and lay at the root of the methods by which the clergy taxed themselves for the service of the Crown. When Papal provisions were most numerous the King and his barons and clerks got their share; when Papal taxation was at its height, more than 90 per cent. of the proceeds were granted to the Crown by the Pope.[1] Appeals to the Roman Curia were useful to everybody. Why, then, should the clergy seek any other way of life? How could they, even if they wished, and they did not

---

[1] 'Of the total yield of tenths paid by the clergy of England and Wales at the papal order during the reign of Edward II the king received nearly 92 per cent. and the papacy eight. Of the total of about £255,000 which Edward secured from subsidies paid to him by the clergy of England and Wales twenty-five per cent. was levied at the grant of the clergy and seventy-five per cent. at the papal order.' Professor W. E. Lunt, in *Haskins Anniversary Essays* (Boston, 1929), p. 182.

wish, to do so? They were not ultramontanists, but were papists. They were not nationalists, but they were very insular and English.

The King and the courts, I have said, made one very important reservation in their accommodating relations with the Curia. They were resolute in resisting any interference with their control of real property, including the rights of advowsons. The privileges of clergy, the jurisdiction in questions of marriage, and the disposition of personal property by will, the rights of visitation and, on the whole, of discipline—these were generally respected or made the subject of agreement. But the control of the advowson, claimed in the Constitutions of Clarendon in 1164, was regarded as fundamental, and round it gathered the claim to lordship, the rejection of foreign jurisdiction, the claims of the laity as against the clergy, and the other forces which led to the ultimate assertion of the sovereignty of the King in Parliament over ecclesiastical affairs. Here, indeed, we may find one of the strongest tendencies in the development of the national state. King and barons successfully asserted their prerogatives and privileges against any Papal interference with their rights of presentation, and in asserting them acquired a livelier consciousness of their significance, and gave a wider meaning to them. A first step was the claim that, historically, benefices and ecclesiastical corporations, though they might draw their life from elsewhere, owed their existence to the benefactions of the Crown and the nobles. A next step, not maintained nor universally taken, but taken by some from time to time, was the assertion of the right to deprive the church of its property, as when in 1404 some knights of the shire suggested that the land of the clergy should for one year be taken into the King's hands for the purposes of the war. It would not be difficult to trace the connexion between such ideas and the objection to the possession of property in England by alien priories or ecclesiastics, to the shipment of money to ecclesiastics across the sea, to ecclesiastical legislation which conflicted with the law of the land, to the claim of the clergy that they were not bound by laws to which they had not assented, and, above all, to the exercise of foreign jurisdiction affecting the rights of the crown and the functions of the royal courts. The terrible weapon of *praemunire*, under whose threat the Reformation settlement was carried through, had its humble beginnings as a method of procedure against elusive persons who defied the jurisdiction of the royal courts in cases where Papal claims to provision had affected royal rights; it was merely subsidiary to the Statute of Provisors, just as the Statute of Provisors was merely intended to strengthen the hands of the royal judges in their administration of the law. This legislation could be and frequently was made inoperative by royal dispensation, if it suited the Crown not to act upon it. Gradually the Statutes of *Praemunire* were interpreted to justify action against the exercise of foreign or private jurisdiction without royal consent. The threat of *praemunire*, with its penalties of deprivation, was used by Henry VIII against the whole clergy on the ground that they had acquiesced in the legatine jurisdiction of Cardinal Wolsey, a jurisdiction which the clergy had cause to detest and which the King had both favoured and helped to procure for the great minister. And the clergy had neither the power nor the temper to resist.

While compromise between ecclesiastical and secular authority had produced an insular complexity in social relationships, it had done nothing to develop, but rather had hindered the possibility of a national religious consciousness. King and clergy alike had freely availed themselves of the Papal power, while resenting, in different ways, arbitrary interference from Rome. Laity and clergy were inextricably involved in a common social system, yet anti-clericalism, in the form of general suspicion rather than of personal class feeling, had grown stronger. The Papacy, driven along by force of circumstances, had in its turn acquiesced in a situation which tended to the advantage of the royal power because it emphasized the independence of the royal courts and the self-consciousness of the laity. By an ironic change of circumstance, the last great Papal legate in England revealed the absence of moral and logical coherence in ecclesiastical society. As one writer has observed, Thomas Cromwell had seen his former master Wolsey 'use his position as cardinal and legate to intercept, as it were, the stream of ecclesiastical administration in its natural course between England and Rome by deciding most of the appeals himself, though always professedly as the Pope's delegate, and thus concentrating in his own hands the power of the Church. The state of things which Wolsey had thus brought about as a temporary phenomenon . . . Cromwell proposed to render permanent and normal', that is to say, by transferring all this power to the King.[1] On the other hand, Wolsey's jurisdiction had alienated the clergy because it had meant daily interference with their administrative powers. Warham, the Archbishop of Canterbury, Bishop Fisher of Rochester, and Sir Thomas More had all disliked or been shocked by the career of the legate. In the document which he signed when he fell from power Wolsey acknowledged that on the authority of bulls obtained by him from Rome he had 'unlawfully vexed the greater number of the prelates of this realm and of the king's subjects, thereby incurring the penalties of praemunire'. He had been clear-sighted enough to see, as time went on, that if he could retain his hold upon the King, the Church in England would be involved in his downfall. He had *not* realized the effect of his policy in weakening such strength and independence as the prelates still possessed. The weapon which

[1] G. W. Child, *Church and State under the Tudors* (London, 1890), pp. 48, 49. This point of view has been taken independently by Professor A. F. Pollard, in his important biography of Wolsey (London, 1929) and worked out more fully; cf. especially p. 215.

was used against him could be used against them, and they found themselves powerless to resist. Indeed, many of the clergy were in fact relieved. They had lost touch with Rome; they could not lose touch with King Henry.

The perplexity of the clergy when they were brought face to face with the great issues raised by the crown must have been great in the extreme. The long-drawn-out discussions about the divorce, the ill feeling aroused by the legation of Wolsey, the conflicts between royal and Papal claims to supremacy, all came together, stirring argument and passion, yet they had no logical coherence with each other. A man might sympathize with Queen Catherine and yet be indifferent to the claims of Rome, or be a strong Papalist and at the same time hope that the King would get his divorce. He might be willing to die for the unity of the Church, yet rejoice in the fall of the Cardinal. And in addition to these issues, drawing them first here, now there, still more distracting, because more subtle, influences were working upon the clergy. These were the days of the 'new learning'. In the more contemptuous speech of the time the new learning was the newfangled teaching brought from Germany and disseminated by a few pernicious books. Making its way with a more powerful impetus than the old Lollard doctrines had ever acquired, it advocated very much the same thing. It upheld the sufficiency of Scripture, drew a distinction between the faithful who formed the true and hidden Church and the 'idolatrous' majority of all grades of learning and position, insisted upon the folly of pilgrimages and image worship and like superstitions. In the days to come, when Protestantism was in power, this new learning was acclaimed by Latimer as really the old learning, the true teaching, and the opprobrious epithet 'new' was hotly repudiated. But we can justly use the phrase in a much wider sense to include these and all the other ideas and tendencies which were influencing the minds of men. At all times of intellectual activity in the history of the Church there have been conflicting cross-currents at work among the clergy and, in growing measure, among the laity; but the cross-currents had never been so many nor the conflict so apparent as in the early years of the sixteenth century. Throughout the fifteenth century there had been much criticism and much apologetic, and the apologetic had sometimes been as provoking as the criticism. No Englishman had criticized the abuses in the Church more fiercely than the rigid conservative Gascoigne, Chancellor of the University of Oxford; no apologist had been so active as the independent-minded bishop of Chichester, Reginald Pecock. And the critic, firm in his orthodoxy, had helped to fasten upon the apologist the charge of heresy, not because he had defended abuses but because in their defence he had surrendered the main position. Both men had hated Lollardy, but denunciation both of Lollards and of the evils which gave plausibility to their views was safer than misguided attempts to convert them. Pecock had relied upon his cleverness rather than upon the tradition secured by the saints of old. In the middle of the fifteenth century it had not been difficult to crush cleverness of his kind; but fifty years later intellectual agility was more common, more varied and subtle, more unchecked. It covered a wider field, so that any man could find arguments to prove the rightness of the things he desired. So we find the nimble-witted king, while never giving himself away, protecting a man who would write on the lawfulness of expropriating the clergy and another who would maintain the principle of absolute sovereignty. It is quite a mistake to suppose that this spirit of independence was confined to one party, for there was no party. Holiness and self-seeking, cleverness and obscurantism can be found side by side among men of all ways of thinking. There was at first little heresy in the new studies at Cambridge, described by Erasmus with such pleasure in a famous letter. Cambridge was to produce the great reforming prelates and divines, but at first the return to the humanities involved no discord between the old faith and reason. Indeed, the suspicion of learning as such was far more apparent among the advocates of the 'new learning' in its narrow heretical sense, and Sir Thomas More, in his *Dialogue concerning Heresies* (1527), used all his ingenuity and wit to show that reason is the servant and not the enemy of faith. This is how he describes the outlook of the messenger with whom he was to discuss:

And thereupon perceiving him to have your sons at school, inquiring further of him, to what faculty he had most given his study, I understood him to have given diligence to the latin tongue. As for other faculties he wrought not of. For he told me merrily that Logic he reckoned for babbling, Music to serve for fingers, Arithmetic meet for merchants, geometry for masons, astronomy good for no man, and as for Philosophy, the most vanity of all, and that it and logic had lost all good divinity with the subtleties of their questions, and babbling of their disputations, *building all upon reason, which rather giveth blindness than any light.* For man (he said) hath no light but of holy scripture.

As we read the history of the time we soon cease to look for any clear-cut divisions or to be surprised by the way a man would think. The career of Henry Standish, Provincial of the Grey Friars, is illuminating. He was a strong churchman, a judge of heretics, a bitter critic of Erasmus, one of the official defenders of Queen Catherine during her so-called trial, and only at the end of his life (1535) showed his readiness to accept the royal supremacy in the Church; yet this description alone would give a very misleading idea of the man. Early in the young king's reign he won favour as a court preacher and became one of Henry's advisers. The Pope made him Bishop of St. Asaph in 1518 to please the King. And he is best known in history for his stand, in 1515, on behalf of the rights of the secular

courts to try the clergy, and to disregard Papal bulls
which were contrary to the public interest. Parliament had
recently renewed a Statute—a temporary measure passed
in 1512—depriving murderers and robbers in minor
orders of benefit of clergy; a well-known abbot, Richard
Kidderminster of Winchcombe, had defended the im-
munity of the clergy in a sermon preached at St. Paul's
Cross. The feeling against clerical privilege was at this
time running high, and in reply the bishops were closing
their ranks. There was nothing new in such a situation: a
wave of anti-clericalism on the one side, a clerical rally on
the other. When the abbot's sermon was brought to his
attention, the King was interested and a discussion was
arranged at Blackfriars, at which Henry and his judges
were present. Standish, the head of the Franciscans in
England and the court preacher, argued the case against
the Benedictine, and here we do feel a new atmosphere.
The public welfare, Standish maintained, was the main
consideration, Papal decrees (and in this instance the
canonical system was involved) had not been received in
England and were often disregarded even by bishops.
Here the old spirit of compromise between ecclesiastical
and spiritual jurisdiction is given higher significance as a
historical fact, vindicating the superior rights of the common well-being. It needed little to turn the argument of
this follower of St. Francis into a claim for royal supremacy.
When convocation proceeded against Standish, ostensibly
on the ground of similar utterances in sermons and lec-
tures, the King went further. The case against him was
again brought out of the control of the clergy to the jurisdiction of king and judges. It needed little more to make
the King the judge in matters of heresy. But here I am not
concerned with the revelation of his prerogative given to
a shrewd young king of twenty-four years of age, but with
the outlook of an orthodox friar of long experience upon
one of the crucial issues in the relations between Church
and State. It helps us to understand the position of a

strong-willed man like Gardiner and the perplexities of Cranmer. For, once latent dilemmas were brought into the open and a decision was forced, it was impossible to rely upon clerical opinion. There was no clear tradition of common action.

For the same reason it is very hard to find one's way in the story of the early trials for heresy. Not very many suffered death. Some heretics were disregarded as harmless cranks, others, doubtless, were protected by their own discretion. Of the two best known, Bilney and Frith, the former was convicted for his attacks upon images and pilgrimages, the general hypocrisy and pride and futility in the Church, the other because of his views on the Mass. 'Little Bilney' became a hero in later Protestant circles; but, considered in the light of the affectionate recollections of his friend Latimer and the pitying but ruthless analysis of his case given by Sir Thomas More, he is a very pathetic figure. He was not at all like the usual disciple of the new learning. He was a curious mixture of self-confidence and timidity, unbalanced yet buoyed up by 'scrupulous holiness'. More says of him 'wherein him liked he set himself at liberty'. He could not remain firm and he could not let things be. Too able and persuasive to be disregarded, he had no stability, yet he was neither a coward nor was he carried away by self-importance. Now sad with servile dread, now uplifted with 'the vain gladness of heart which he took for spiritual consolation', first recanting, then tormented by conscience, he seems to reflect the perplexity of his time, as the cross-currents of life swept over his serious and sensitive but puzzled soul. Strange echoes of apocalyptic fury against the Papacy, the powerful impression made by Tyndale's writings, hatred of idolatrous roods and dainty singing and all the pomp and vanity of clerical life mingled with his firm belief in the central dogmas of the Church. A sense of helpless dependence upon the Church fought with his passion for preaching and his certainty of the experience which he

had found in the Scriptures. And so in 1531, after re-
ceiving much consideration, he was burned as a relapsed
heretic. He is so significant because he was so much better
than the people about him. He could not merely be
critical and cynical, and shrug his shoulders or take up
one popular cry after another. He was not, like so many
medieval heretics of his type, an exception in a world
which was sure of itself; he was an exceptionally serious
man in a world which was not sure of itself and yet did not
much care, because it was conscious of the strength and
energy and freedom in itself, a world in which cruelty and
cynicism had free play, and indifference did not matter,
yet a world in which self-assertiveness was almost in-
distinguishable from the craving after experience, whether
of beauty or adventure or sheer evil. It was an exciting,
though very dangerous, time for the men with ideas, and a
good time for those who wanted to see what would hap-
pen. Sir Thomas More, secure in the citadel of his well-
ordered integrity, was not quite just to the people who
found life very perplexing, but he does remind us of the
element of self-importance and excitement always to be
found among the reformers in such an age as his; he saw
very little good in the 'ardent appetite to preach' and tells
of one of the new kind of preachers who attributed bad
preaching to the lack of persecution. This man wished to
see strife and business arise upon their preaching. 'The
fruit of strife among the hearers and persecution of the
preacher cannot lightly grow among Christian men but by
the preaching of some strange novelties and bringing up of
some newfangled heresies to the infection of our old faith.'
He knew a man who, after being convinced of error, was
filled with such an open passion of shame when he came
among the people who held him in esteem, that he revoked his revocation. After a time, the books which had
convinced him of error were brought to him again, and he
himself read them before the people 'so that he perceived
the audience that stood about him to feel and understand

his proud folly'. So he yielded himself again. 'Such secret pride had our ghostly enemy conveyed in to the heart of him, which, I ensure you, seemed in all his other outward manners as meek a simple soul as a man should have seen in a summer's day.'

II. THE DISSOLUTION OF THE MONASTERIES

THIS atmosphere of uncertainty and unrest is felt at once when we turn to the monastic life. The fall of the monasteries (1536–40) comes later in the first stage of ecclesiastical revolution, but its story is so closely linked with what had gone before and with the intangible changes of thought and outlook in society that it may appropriately be discussed here. No aspect of the Reformation has been so hotly and inconclusively debated, yet no one, whatever view he may take, would deny that in a perplexing age this is the most perplexing of subjects. The evidence itself is as perplexing as it is extensive. The historian cannot form from it a coherent impression of what the monks thought about the change, nor of what their neighbours thought. Some well-documented books have been written which give us a picture of a popular healthy element in social and religious society, mysteriously crushed out of existence by greed. Other equally well-documented books give us a picture of a corrupt survival in the body politic cut away to the general relief. Both kinds of book tend to heighten the dramatic quality of their story by giving it in a setting of excitement and passion, as though an exotic and morbid experience had disturbed the national life. Yet, if we try to look at the passing of the monasteries as a whole, we get quite a different impression. The great change, involving the extinction of about 550 houses and the dispersion of some 7,000 religious (excluding the friars), was carried through in characteristic English fashion. It was exceedingly business-like, yet not pedantic, smooth in some places, rough in others, comic here and tragic there, but generally humdrum and unsentimental. There was little physical disturbance with the life of the shires, and far less scrambling for land or displacement of local interest than is usually supposed. The monks got livings or pensions, many of the abbots and priors became secular dignitaries and ended their days as bishops and deans. The financial transactions required for the raising of the purchase price of such an extensive mass of property—for most of the monastic lands were sold at their estimated value—no doubt involved social changes which have not yet been adequately explored; but it would seem that the country gentry, who were more familiar with the properties and had helped to manage them, as often as not succeeded in buying them. The percentage of arable land was high, and the lay element which had served the monastic establishments would, on the whole, not find much difficulty in finding employment.

This description may sound surprising, and in any case requires some amplification if it is not to be misleading. It is important to bear in mind the nature of the monastic economy and also the methods of which the State could avail itself in the work of centralized supervision. The connexion between the monasteries and the neighbouring laity had always been very close. I have already had occasion to observe that in the three previous centuries the barons and gentry had frequently insisted upon their part in the creation of ecclesiastical endowments; and their feeling that they had not lost all control of the gifts of their ancestors was as strong in their attitude to the regular as it was in their attitude to the secular clergy. It was recognized in some measure at the time of the dissolution—the representatives of founders and donors were secured in their right to retain any fixed income still payable to them—and it was not overlooked by the great commentators on the common law. But in the nature of things argument of this kind was largely a political gesture and had little relation to facts in the beginning of the sixteenth century. The share taken by the neighbouring laity in the actual administration of monastic property and the consequent intimacy of social relations between the monasteries and the local inhabitants were much more important. Some great noblemen, such as the duke of Suffolk and the earl of Shrewsbury, acted through their officials as stewards of half a dozen or more monasteries, and in most cases a county gentleman of standing held this position. The auditors, receivers, and bailiffs were usually laymen. A great part of the monastic lands were leased to laymen. On the other hand, in return for definitely arranged benefactions, laymen might be received into the monastery or their children brought up within its walls. Local gentry, for years before the dissolution, had been given monastic advowsons as unacknowledged trustees, under an obligation to present monks, who had received their 'capacities', to the livings as incumbents. The transition to the new order was made easy by this traditional concern of the laity in monastic affairs. The 'spoliation' did not imply a cataclysm so much as an infinite series of adjustments. If a layman received a monastery as a gift from the Crown he was responsible for the pensions of the monks, and in some cases he had to pay even more than he got in annual revenue. Moreover, examination of the financial survey has shown that the number of laymen dependent upon the monasteries and the amount of 'charity' which the monks administered has been over-estimated. Just as many of the monks and nuns were of wealthy or gentle origin, so were many of their pensioners. At the most thirty-five thousand laymen were fed in monasteries, including the officials and servants who could find employment elsewhere. The amount of alms officially recognized, and therefore free from taxation, was about 3 per cent. of the monastic budget, and this was mainly expended in food for the poor who gathered on fixed days in the year. The dissolution must have caused much suffering and inconvenience, but it did not create a proletariat. The distress must have varied greatly in different parts of the country, in some places hardly noticeable, severe in others—especially in the lonely places where the hospitality of the monks was a real boon to travellers, and monastic ministrations to the poor were their only alleviation. The social significance of a big abbey in a wild and thinly populated area was one thing, the value to the community of a group of houses, of all sizes and shades of decrepitude, in a busy and well-populated shire was a very different thing. The seven thousand persons under monastic vows were scattered in tiny communities among a population of three or four million. Their economic interests were interlocked with those of their neighbours and were in the main administered by laymen.

If the disposal of the monastic lands and houses had been left to local control there would doubtless have been more give and take than there was. In many places the monks had the goodwill of their neighbours and so far as was possible were shown consideration. Even Latimer, the bishop of Worcester, had his friends among them and spoke up on behalf of men who, apart from their 'monkery', could still take a valuable part in local life if they were allowed to retain their positions under different conditions. But such a method of dealing with the problem would have had great disadvantages: it would have involved more suffering, intrigue, and scrambling for wealth, a struggle long drawn out between conflicting interests. In any case, it was quite impossible, for the suppression of the monasteries was a great act of State—the first assertion on a large scale by the Tudor monarchy of its competence to put parliamentary legislation in domestic affairs into action. The first stage in the dissolution was contemporary with the absorption of Papal into royal interests in the financial administration of the Church.

The abolition of the annates or first-fruits, the payments made to the Papal Curia on all sorts of occasions, as a result of papal provision to prelacies and benefices,[1] had been

---

[1] By this time the term 'annates' was used to comprise both annates proper, paid by clergy papally provided to benefices of a certain value, and the older 'services' paid by prelates to Pope and Cardinals, when for various reasons they had been appointed in consistory, i.e. by Pope and Cardinals.

B

effected in 1534, in accordance with a Statute of 1532, and
had been demanded by clergy and laity alike. But in the
next year, 1535, after the royal supremacy had been
secured (Nov. 1534), the King's right to these payments
was declared. They were extended to all benefices and at
the same time ecclesiastical taxes or tenths were made
annual and permanent. This change was accompanied by
a commission of inquiry into all ecclesiastical revenues—a
new and exhaustive assessment which in its operation was
very like the Papal investigations of the thirteenth century
which hitherto had been the basis of ecclesiastical taxation
by King and Pope. The result was the valuation returns
which were worked up into the famous *Valor Ecclesiasticus*.
Hence, when in 1535 the great visitation of the monasteries
was undertaken under the supervision of Thomas Cromwell, the King's Vicar-General for ecclesiastical affairs,
the Crown had already in its possession a survey of
monastic wealth and was using for the material control of
the whole Church all the machinery of government, all
the experience acquired by exchequer and chancery
during the previous centuries. King Henry had convinced
himself that, if he were not the source of doctrine, he was
the judge in all things ecclesiastical, could appoint and deprive bishops, say what doctrine was right and what
wrong, reform the Canon Law, and, through Parliament,
control the property of the clergy. The dissolution of the
smaller monasteries, which followed Cromwell's visitation, was the most drastic expression ever seen in England
of the new theory of the secular state. By the Act of 1536
(27 Henry VIII, c. 28) the actual and real possessions of
all the monastic houses 'which have not in lands, tene-
ments, rents, tithes, portions, and hereditaments, above the
clear yearly value of two hundred pounds' passed into the
King's hands. The vested interests in fixed payments and
offices were secured, the claims of creditors were to be
satisfied, the heads of houses and the monks and nuns provided for; but no other proprietary rights than those of the

Crown were to be permitted. In one respect this Statute may justly be said to signify an important advance in the development of the sovereignty of King in Parliament. Hitherto, when property for any reason fell to the Crown, the King could not acquire or enjoy his legal title until a local jury had allowed it (Statutes 8 Henry VI, c. 16, and 18 Henry VI, c. 6). If the new Statute had been vaguely worded, all sorts of claims to ownership in the religious houses might well have arisen to restrain the rights of the Crown. The Act of Parliament would have become the subject of discussion in the courts, to be interpreted in the light of other evidence and the rules of common law. But Henry and his advisers had anticipated this contingency. It is probable that the isolated and rather mysterious surrender in 1532 of the important priory of Austin Canons at Aldgate, in London, was designed or at least used to secure the position of the King.[1] A special Act of Parliament confirmed the procedure of surrender and gave Henry and his successors full enjoyment of the property, 'as though office and offices had been duly found thereof according to the laws of this realm', that is to say, the Statutes of Henry VI. In Fuller's phrase, the confiscation 'shrewdly shook the freehold of all abbeys'. However this may be, in the Act of 1536 the rights of others than the King were definitely excluded, and 'such as pretend to be founders, patrons, and donors' were, in company with abbots and other governors of religious houses, excluded from all rights or interests other than such fixed annual payments as practice allowed them. The supremacy of the King in Parliament was secured, and henceforth any purchaser or grantee of monastic lands had a secure title from the Crown. The returns in the *Valor Ecclesiasticus* were supplemented by careful local investigation into the value of all property so disposed of, and the entire administration

---

[1] See the important paper by Miss Jeffries Davis, 'The Beginning of the Dissolution', in *The Transactions of the Royal Historical Society*, Fourth Series, viii (1925), 127–50.

of this new wealth of the Crown was vested in a new department, the Court of Augmentations, and ultimately in the Exchequer. Although much intrigue and corruption infected this administration, it was carried on with all the minute care which had become second nature in the departments of state. The valuations were recorded in detail, and the local officials of the Augmentation office paid the pensions of the dispossessed monks in due form every half year. How carefully the whole transaction had been considered appears from the clause in the Act that future owners or lessees of monastic property should be bound, under penalties, to keep 'an honest continual house and household in the same site or precinct, and to occupy yearly as much of the same demesnes in ploughing and tillage of husbandry'. But in this respect continuity of the domestic economy and hospitality of the monasteries was too much to be hoped for. The temptation to buy monastic lands in the hope of a profit, either by selling again or by rack-renting or recourse to more remunerative methods of exploitation, was very often too severe. The new owners had generally paid a full price, and must have included in their numbers many strangers and new capitalists. It is very easy to exaggerate the effect of the dissolution in hastening economic change, for the monasteries had naturally had no clear policy of their own, and this change had widespread causes, quite independent of the monastic economy. But the transfer of so much land and local interest to laymen whose rights were protected by the Crown and were dependent upon the new settlement in Church and State did much to shake the traditional order of things, to break down the old connexions in local life, and to give a powerful vested interest in the maintenance of the royal supremacy.

As an annihilation of ancient rights, the Dissolution of the Monasteries was an act of absolute power; but it was not an act of irresponsible power. It was part of a sweeping reconstruction of the Church in England. There is some evidence for the belief that not long before the King had played with the idea of a general spoliation of the Church, in which salaried bishops and clergy, as in modern France, would have taken their place beside the pensioned religious. When it is regarded as part of a wide plan for the development of educational and social services, as the idealists like Latimer desired, and for the reorganization of the diocesan system, as was in fact in part achieved by the foundation of the new bishoprics of Westminster, Gloucester, Oxford and Chester, Peterborough and Bristol, and by a large increase in the number of suffragan bishops, this bold scheme had real merit; but performance lagged far behind the promise to convert monastic wealth to better uses, and it was a good thing that the plan for a general confiscation did not come to anything. It was too revolutionary in the sixteenth, as it had been in the fifteenth century. Yet at a time when such proposals could be seriously discussed, and when so much was accomplished, it is as misleading to isolate the Dissolution as a piece of wanton tyranny, as it is misleading to isolate the monks from their neighbours and to regard them as immune from the influence of current opinion. The fall of the smaller monasteries helped to precipitate the movement in Lincolnshire and the north of England, known as the Pilgrimage of Grace (1536), just as the Act of Uniformity in Edward VI's reign (1549) brought the discontent in the west of England to a head; but it is quite clear that the Pilgrimage of Grace, rightly described by Mr. Fisher as a demonstration rather than a rebellion, was directed against the 'new learning' and the injunctions and interference of the Vicar-General as much as against the Dissolution. In England as a whole there was excitement, and much consternation, but no opposition. Nor, on the other hand, was there any widespread indignation against the monastic orders and the monks. The horror of monastic depravity which is expressed in the Act of 1535 was not a true reflection of popular opinion. The revelations of Cromwell's unsavoury commissioners were discounted by the findings of the commission which administered the Act. There had always been laxity in the monastic life since the first enthusiasm had passed. The revelations of episcopal visitations in the fifteenth century are very like those of the thirteenth, and the state of the monasteries in 1535 was, if we consider only grave scandals, probably not much worse. If there had been widespread sympathy with monastic aims, there is no reason why drastic reform—the elimination of tiny and useless houses, the grouping of others, the revision and enforcements of the Rules—should not have taken the place of abolition. Proposals of this kind had been in the air for a generation. Wolsey and others had made a beginning with Papal approval. The injunctions of the commissioners themselves seemed to contemplate reform. The success of Abbot Kidderminster's organization of monastic studies at Winchcombe showed that much could be made of the existing system. A strong king, supported by a determined episcopate, might have carried through with infinitely greater effect the kind of reform which was attempted in the Cluniac Order by John of Bourbon, bishop of Puy and abbot of Cluny, in the second half of the fifteenth century. But it is clear that the desire was lacking, both within and without the monasteries. There was no very strong feeling against them except among the Reformers; the neighbourly instincts which prompt men to dislike change would, if they had been undisturbed, have been sufficient to protect them, but there was little strong belief in them and no intention of fighting for them. And within their walls, when the issue was once raised, and the bearing of the royal policy was realized, there was in most places no closing of the ranks, no passion of opposition. Rather, old feuds and differences and jealousies were enlarged and embittered. The 'new learning' had itself penetrated into some abbeys and was influencing the younger monks. The new 'lecturers' introduced by bishops like Latimer had added to the confusion. There was general reluctance to move, and the majority undoubtedly disliked the trend of events, but they were demoralized by uncertainty, made fearful by gossip and intrigue among themselves. They found it wiser to come to terms, to look out for livings, or take their pensions. The abbots and priors were comfortably provided for; a dozen or so became bishops, others suffragans, others the deans of the cathedral chapters of secular clergy into which their old foundations—Carlisle, Durham, Ely, Norwich, Rochester, Winchester—were converted. Some married and founded county families, on the strength of their pluralities. Their monks followed suit, as incumbents or pensioners, and several of them still survived at the end of Elizabeth's reign, like the veterans of the Crimea or the Mutiny in our own time.

This is no story of wholesale flights oversea, still less of thumb-screws and priests' holes. It is just that of a great company of Englishmen and Englishwomen, faced suddenly with a great crisis in their lives, setting to work, grumbling and growling, to make the best of a bad business, and to ensure their future by all the means available to them; the story, not of what ecclesiastical gladiators would have them to do, but of what the overwhelming majority of them did.[1]

One of the most far-reaching effects of the Dissolution was the passage into private hands of the rights of presentation to churches of which the monasteries had possessed the advowson. At the time some of the monks had the benefit of these rights; as the century passed, new generations of clergy were provided by the new patrons. The survival and extension of the private advowson gave an independence to the parish clergy during the changes of opinion in ecclesiastical and theological matters which

[1] G. Baskerville, 'The Dispossessed Religious after the Suppression of the Monasteries', in *Essays in History presented to Reginald Lane Poole* (Oxford, 1927), p. 465. In the preceding account I have depended very much on this admirable paper, and on the work of A. Savine, 'English Monasteries on the eve of the Dissolution', in the *Oxford Studies in Social and Legal History*, i (1909).

should not be overlooked. A Puritan patron would tend to appoint a Puritan vicar. A country squire would not think first of episcopal wishes or policy. The relations between the laity and the clergy were strengthened and the prospects of uniformity in clerical opinion diminished by the transference of property from the religious houses to the gentry.

The real tragedy in the story of the Dissolution must be sought, not in any dramatic conflict between the powers of good and evil, but in the very perplexities which assailed the monastic population. Hidden away among the indifferent were the troubled, and among the troubled were the saints and idealists and the few men of iron will. These were the true sufferers, whether they sought for a compromise which they could not find, or stood out firmly for Papal Supremacy and a united church, and above all, for the ideal of the religious life, the life of men who dedicate themselves to prayer for sinful and suffering mankind. These men, who were hanged at Tyburn or at their abbey gates, were the martyrs, for they felt about the monastic rule as Sir Thomas More felt. At the very least they could not conceal, in a chattering and malicious world, the faith that was in them. Some, like the brave Carthusians, were heroic men; others, like the unhappy Abbot Hobbes of Woburn, were weak men.[1] 'Brethren, this is a parlous time. Such a scourge was never heard sith Christ's Passion.' But if all had felt as they did, the Pilgrimage of Grace would have been a national, an irresistible movement. As things were, the greater monasteries followed the lesser or were transferred into secular cathedrals.

[1] See the very moving story of Abbot Hobbes in Gairdner, *Lollardy and the Reformation*, ii. 133–40.

III. FROM THE LEGISLATION OF HENRY VIII TO THE SECOND PRAYER BOOK OF EDWARD VI

THE secularization of the extensive properties of the monasteries and the creation of a government office to administer the disposal of them raised the question of the rights of property as against the right of the State. By giving a nip to the abbeys, Henry did a great deal to set men's minds towards the theory of the State as a sovereign power, rather than as a self-directed organism held together by a common regard for customary rights and obligations. Most good men were in agreement upon the moral issue. They regretted the loss of the opportunity to convert ecclesiastical property to religious uses, which in their eyes included social and educational uses, although most monastic property was, of course, essentially secular in character and always subject in England to the common law. Latimer, as is well known, held this view, and Cranmer in the end of Edward VI's reign resisted the wanton spoliation of the Church. But by this time the greed of Northumberland and his satellites was but part of a policy which would have destroyed the traditional status of the Church of England and might well have involved its ultimate reconstruction on a non-episcopal basis, as abhorrent to Ridley and Cranmer as it was to Gardiner and Bonner. Cranmer, although he voted with most of the other bishops against the confiscation of the chantries and colleges in 1547, did not share the view of the Cambridge divine, Miles Wilson, that the seizure of ecclesiastical property was impious.[1] One of the articles of the rebels of

---

[1] Wilson reduced the arguments of his Cambridge oration *De rebus ecclesiae non diripiendis* to the form of a syllogistic summary and sent it by request to his acquaintance, William Cecil, at that time already one of the secretaries of State, in 1552; this is printed in Strype's *Memorials of Cranmer* (edited 1854), iii, 651–9.

Devon in 1549 asked for the restoration of the half part of the abbey lands and chantry land in every man's possession, however, he came by them, 'to be given again to two places, where two of the chief abbeys were within every county; where such half part shall be taken out, and there to be established a place for devout persons, which shall pray for the King and the Commonwealth'. In his reply to the articles Cranmer dealt very firmly with this suggestion:

At the beginning you pretended that you meant nothing against the King's Majesty, but now you open yourselves plainly to the world that you go about to pluck the crown from his head; and, against all justice and equity not only to take from him such lands as be annexed unto his crown, and be parcel of the same, but also against all right and reason to take from all other men such lands as they came to by most just title, by gift, by sale, by exchange, or otherwise. There is no respect nor difference had amongst you, whether they came to them by right or by wrong. Be you so blind that you cannot see how justly you proceed to take the sword into your hands against your prince, and to dispossess just inheritors without any cause? Christ would not take upon him to judge the right and title of lands between two brethren; and you arrogantly presume not only to judge, but unjustly to take away all men's right titles; yea, even from the King himself.

Now, when he spoke of right titles, the archbishop was obviously referring to the rights given or covered by the King in Parliament. It was not for the rebels to question the fact, when the fact had legal sanction. And this brings us to a much wider issue than that of the right to the abbey lands. Was this breach with the past characteristic of the Reformation settlement in England as a whole? Or, to put the point in a different way, was the reorganization of the Church by Parliament regarded as inconsistent with the maintenance of its continuity? Did it substitute for a divine right the rights implied in a secular sanction? We can most profitably study the history of the Reformation with this issue in our minds. We are not concerned with the reflections of later ecclesiastics and theologians upon it, but with the facts, and, an essential element among the facts, the views of the chief actors in the movement about what they were doing or trying to do or preventing others from doing.

As is well known, formal continuity was maintained in England to a degree without parallel in any other reformed country with the exception of Sweden. Episcopal government, the assembly of the clergy in convocations and synods, the general diocesan system, the method of exercising discipline, and for twenty years the rites and ceremonies which had developed in the past to give expression to the doctrine of the Church, all these were retained. Moreover, until the latter part of Edward VI's reign, and in spite of acute differences of opinion, ecclesiastical life in England presented a picture of unity. This was doubtless due very largely to the strong personality of King Henry VIII, but Henry was helped by opinion. There were no Catholic recusants, no Protestant dissenters. A few died as traitors because they denied the royal supremacy, a few more were burned as heretics because they rejected some of the dogmas or teaching of the Catholic Church. During all the changes effected before the second Act of Uniformity of 1552 there were very few people who were indifferent to the maintenance of the existing order. Thomas Cromwell was probably the only exception among the persons of influence; and it is significant that he was attainted as a 'detestable heretic' as well as a traitor. When it was seen that the spread of foreign opinions and the public discussions about the Mass were producing a state of ferment in which violence and blasphemy could find free expression, there was a general revulsion of feeling. Protestant bishops, Cranmer, Ridley, Latimer, and such advanced reformers as Bradford and Knox were alarmed. Queen Mary had the benefit of the reaction. This conservatism was rooted in an instinct of self-preservation, it was the natural result of the confusion in which medieval compromising and the peculiar conditions of English life had left the relations between Church and State. Englishmen were ready to do without the Pope, but were prepared for nothing else. Nobody in those days had any clear-cut theory of what the English Church was; indeed, it is hardly too much to say that nobody with the exception of Cranmer was sure what the 'Church of England' was. Ecclesiastical jurisdiction was haphazard and chaotic, and Cranmer tried in vain to get recognition of a definite system of ecclesiastical law. The precise share of Convocation in the deliberations which preceded the chief measures of this time, for example the first Act of Uniformity and the official publication of the First Prayer Book of Edward VI, is one of the most debatable problems in the history of the Reformation. Here lies the chief difference between the developments in the reign of Henry VIII and Edward VI and the settlement under Queen Elizabeth. During Elizabeth's reign the system of ecclesiastical administration, although it left much room for royal and parliamentary intervention, was at least coherent. The English Church found its apologists and exponents in Parker, Jewel, Hooker, Whitgift, and Bancroft. On the other hand, religious life in England was anything but united. Opposition came not from a few heretics but from groups of men, mainly within the Church, who preferred an entirely different system and cared nothing for continuity. And the second breach with Rome forced an issue, as clear-cut as it had been blurred in King Henry's time, between the Roman and the English views of the Church. The events of Queen Mary's reign had made this inevitable.

We must first deal with the earlier period, which culminated in the disputes about the Second Prayer Book of Edward VI.

The Reformation in England was a parliamentary transaction. All the important changes were made under statutes, and the actions of the King as supreme head of the

Church were done under a title and in virtue of powers given to him by statute. Disciplinary action was administered, whether by the civil courts, special commissions, or the ecclesiastical authorities, according to rules laid down in statutes or in virtue of authority allowed by the King in Parliament. As a general rule proposed changes were first submitted to Convocation or to a group of advisers, who were sometimes a mixed body of ecclesiastics and laymen, sometimes ecclesiastics alone; but any preliminary discussions or decisions of Convocation or advisers required parliamentary sanction or royal approval. The bishops continued to issue injunctions and articles of visitation, but any general action, even if it were concerned with doctrinal change or ritual, required secular sanctions. If the leaders or synods of the Church had attempted any changes without such sanctions they would have been liable to proceedings involving the pains and penalty of praemunire, that 'purely English word', as the Milanese ambassador amusingly described it.[1] They would have acted upon or acknowledged an alien jurisdiction in matters affecting the interests of the crown and kingdom. Hence came the reluctance of the bishops to move a step unless they could carry the secular authorities with them and have legal protection for everything that they did. Nobody felt the necessity of this more strongly than that

---

[1] In 1530; see Pollard, *Wolsey*, p. 249. The word was originally simply a form of forewarning in a writ of procedure, beginning *praemunire facias*. The forewarning 'supplied a new name for the statute out of which it had grown', the statute of 1353 (E. B. Graves in *Haskins Anniversary Essays*, p. 75). The so-called great statute of *Praemunire* (1393) was an application of this procedure against offenders who sought process in the Court of Rome or elsewhere in particular kinds of cases which, as was admitted by the clergy, affected the royal jurisdiction. In course of time this statute was interpreted to cover all recourse to any jurisdiction infringing on that of the crown. See W. T. Waugh in the *English Historical Review*, xxxvii (1922), 173–205, and Pollard's *Wolsey*. Wolsey, Mr. Pollard observes, was an adept in its use, but was indicted under it. The most powerful inpersonation of Papal jurisdiction in England was condemned 'by a simple and almost routine process in the court of King's Bench'. That the King had personally aided and abetted his jurisdiction did not legally help him.

very typical Englishman, Stephen Gardiner; and nobody rejoiced in it more than Thomas Cranmer.

Obviously the first step was to secure recognition of the royal supremacy, for this would *ipso facto* rule out any debate or dispute about the limits to the legal intervention by the courts with a view to preventing the exercise in England of Papal or any other ecclesiastical jurisdiction. During the negotiations with Pope Clement VII about the divorce, Stephen Gardiner, one of the royal envoys, had threatened the Pope. At Orvieto, on the Friday before Palm Sunday, 1528, Gardiner, after a hot discussion, desired the Cardinals to note and ponder such words as he should say 'of duty and obedience towards the See Apostolic'. The Kings and nobles of England might well come to consider that Papal laws which were not clear to the Pope himself nor to his advisers might well be given to the flames. The failure to reach a conclusion in the following year when Wolsey and Campeggio sat as Papal commissioners in England, brought the question to a head. The great cardinal fell, and died on the 29 November 1530. A few days after Wolsey's death the Attorney-General filed an injunction in the Court of King's Bench against the whole body of the clergy. They had recognized the legatine authority of the cardinal and had come within the scope of praemunire. Parliament and Convocation were sitting, and the latter was made to understand that the clergy could make their peace with the King if they would recognize him to be the sole protector and supreme head of the Church in England. The Upper House debated for three days, under the presidency of the archbishop. Finally it silently concurred in the new title 'as far as the law of Christ allows'. The Convocation of the northern province followed suit. This declaration had as yet no clear legal effect. Although the King was already playing with the view that the headship of the Pope had no scriptural or historical validity, and there was much talk about the matter, Henry had no immediate intention of breaking with Rome. He was declared to be head of the Church in England, not of a separate church; but the way was prepared for a further submission of the clergy, and for the first statutory action against Papal rights.

In 1532 Parliament entered on the scene. It is customary to say that Henry VIII's parliaments were entirely subservient to him, a statement which is due in great measure to a misunderstanding of the nature of this assembly in the early sixteenth century. Then, as in the later Middle Ages, it was the highest expression of the King's court. Its legislative enactments had supreme validity, although even a century later the view was still held by the common lawyers that a statute was not invariably to be regarded as binding upon the courts of law. It was the source of taxation. On the other hand, it was not essential to government, it had no privileges except those which attached to its members as men called to serve the Crown, and its business was prepared for and presented to it by the King's ministers. The elected element known as the Commons, who deliberated separately, was closely bound up with the aristocratic society of the shires. Parliament was a gathering for special purposes, to express the common consent of King and people, to ventilate grievances and provide the means of government. Latimer, in one of his sermons, likens it to the day of the second coming of Christ:

This day will be like unto a parliament. Ye know, when things are amiss in a realm, or out of order, all they that be good-hearted, that love godliness, they wish for a parliament; these would fain have that all the rulers of the realm should come together, and bring all things in good order again. For ye know that parliaments are kept only for this purpose, that things which be amiss may be amended.

Hence, if we are to consider the subserviency of Parliament, we must put our modern conceptions on one side. As a matter of fact, Henry, by carrying Parliament with him at every step, during a critical period in our history, gave it a more important place in the commonwealth than it had previously possessed. The very fact that he could not do without it, that no man, however despotic in temper, could afford to break with Rome and reduce the clergy to subjection apart from it, is a tribute to its importance. If there was grumbling and hot speech in the Commons, then a wise king would be very wary, for these people did not readily incur the royal displeasure. A wise king would not act as though there were any necessary cleavage between him and his people; and there is enough evidence to show that the statutes of the reign were not passed without careful debate, and that the King's wishes were not always complied with. Henry managed his parliaments, but he realized the truth of the words spoken by Sir Thomas More as Speaker of the Commons in 1523, that many who are boisterous and rude in language are deep, and he assumed the good faith of the petition that he should interpret every man's words as 'proceeding out of a good zeal towards the profit of your realm and honour of your royal person'. He made heavy calls upon Parliament and knew, as was said during a period of strain in 1531, that his strength lay in the affection of his people.

Wolsey's old servant Thomas Cromwell was sworn a member of the Council in 1530 and was rapidly rising in the royal favour. It was possibly he who saw that the best way to shake the clergy was to array the laity against them. The old Archbishop Warham had already repented of his acquiescence in the royal demands of 1530, and in February 1532 issued a solemn protest which shows something of the spirit of Becket and Grosseteste. It was not difficult to bring anti-clerical feeling to a head. Feeling of this kind was not prevalent in everyday life, but it was easily stirred against the harassing discipline and petty exactions of the Church, and was responsive to mass appeals against ecclesiastical abuses. In 1487 Convocation had included among the matters which required reform the denunciatory sermons of preachers at St. Paul's Cross who would attack the Church, that is to say, its abuses, in the absence of clergy but in the presence of laymen 'qui semper clericis sunt infesti'. In Henry VIII's early years, when excitement about religious matters was still more prevalent, especially in London and other centres of population, ecclesiastical jurisdiction had met with violent criticism. This was very evident in the notorious case of Richard Hunne in 1514. Again, Englishmen, however orthodox, were not uninfluenced by the secular tendencies in continental politics, notably in Germany. As the King's own actions showed, the advantages of secular control would become accepted as a matter of course; the question was in the air. This was the teaching of Tindale, whose books were circulated widely in secret. In 1529 the pamphleteer Simon Fish, and in 1532 a much more respectable person, the lawyer Christopher St. Germain, made it an issue of open debate. St. Germain, in his *Treatise concerning the division between the Spirituality and the Temporality*, while appearing to deplore the situation, drew an extravagant picture of society divided into two hostile camps, and called for the abolition of clerical privileges as harmful to the community. His methods of controversy aroused Sir Thomas More, always an apostle of the natural harmony of society, to protest in hot indignation. All the prevalent movements of thought and feeling are focused with great skill in the petition of the Commons presented to the King in March 1532 and sent on by him to Convocation for reply. Henry adopted an attitude of impartial detachment, but while there is no reason to doubt that the petition expressed the mind of the Commons, it was certainly prepared in the Court. Four corrected drafts of it survive, carefully corrected, and most of the corrections are in the hand of Thomas Cromwell. The rapid growth of fantastical and erroneous opinions, and the dangers of discord and debate provoked by the extreme and uncharitable behaviour of certain ordinaries (or ecclesiastical authorities), are given as the occasion of

the protest. The people are described as subject to ordinances of Convocation, made without royal consent,
and hidden away in a language which they cannot understand. They are pictured as distracted by vexatious delays, exactions, and interference, and caught in a mesh
of unintelligible subtleties and simoniacal practices. Even
those accused of heresy have no chance, attacked without
good reason, exposed to public contempt if they escape, or
as 'some simple silly soul precisely standing to the clear
testimony of his own well-known conscience, rather than
to confess his innocent truth', utterly destroyed. The
moral is drawn that disturbance or unrest cannot be
checked by the pedantic and harsh entanglements of
spiritual discipline. The King should provide redress and
reform, for he is 'the only head, sovereign lord, protector,
and defender of both the said parties'.

This first demonstration of the laity in Parliament is very
significant. It is a skilful appeal to very natural human
feeling, always more powerful than the weighty assertion
of political doctrine. It assumes that the value of an expedient use of the secular authority far outweighs in importance the maintenance of the traditional co-operation
of Church and State. The reply was dignified and able,
but it had no effect, and was the first and last attempt by an
independent Convocation to urge the necessity under
changing conditions of maintaining the conception of an
organic and self-controlled ecclesiastical system, a system
acting with that of the secular authority. It was drawn up
by the new bishop of Winchester, Stephen Gardiner, the
ablest canonist of his time. Gardiner, who like Cromwell
had been in Wolsey's service, had become the King's
Secretary and his chief adviser. He had, as we have seen,
been ardent in promoting the royal divorce and had
warned the Pope that vacillation might involve the repudiation by England of Papal laws. His promotion to the
great see of Winchester at the end of 1531 might well have
been a step to Canterbury. Whether or not he was ig-

norant of the origin of the Commons' petition is not known, but now he had no hesitation in showing that his view of the future was very different from Cromwell's. Gardiner was by temperament and training a constitutionalist. He regarded the maintenance of legal forms as essential to the life and well-being of society, whether in Church or State, and had no belief in arbitrary opportunism. In the reply which he drafted for Convocation he came at once to the crucial issue. All the detailed objections made by the Commons were argued, but they were subsidiary and could be met by simple measures of reform. The essential thing was to maintain the co-operation of the two powers, 'a most sure and perfect conjunction and agreement, as God being *lapis angularis* to agree and conjoin the same'. Let each power temper its own laws with a view to mutual understanding; but the authority of Convocation was grounded upon the Scripture of God and the determination of Holy Church. Its members had a charge and duty entrusted to them by God, and could not submit their execution to the King's assent. Gardiner is often regarded as a hypocrite and time-server, but he was nothing of the sort. Although complete severance from Rome was not yet contemplated by the clergy, and probably was not desired by Henry himself, Gardiner saw no inconsistency between his traditional view of ecclesiastical independence and the acknowledgement of the royal supremacy. He had to give in, but, after he had accepted the logical result of royal supremacy, he stood none the less for the constitutional view of development and for the retention of the old order and the old doctrine in a Church under the control of King and Parliament. But we must return to him later.

In May of this year, 1532, Convocation submitted. Relying on the King's religious zeal and great learning, the clergy promised that they would promulgate or execute no ordinance unless by royal consent. They begged him to appoint a commission of thirty-two persons, of whom sixteen should be clergy and sixteen 'of the upper and nether house of the temporalty', to revise existing constitutions and to bring them into accord with God's law and the laws of the realm.

The final step was delayed for two years. In 1532 Henry was still troubled about the divorce. He had to give up all hope of Papal action in his favour and was threatened with excommunication if he married again, yet if he broke too violently or suddenly with Rome, he might not be able to rely upon the acquiescence of his people. Disturbance at home would mean serious danger from abroad. At this juncture he was able to enlist a new recruit, more cautious, sincere, and respectable than the invaluable Cromwell. This was Thomas Cranmer, who in his fortieth year (1529) had risen with unusual rapidity into prominence. The son of a country gentleman in Nottinghamshire, bred in country sports and an intrepid horseman, Cranmer had gone to Cambridge. After an early but brief marriage he was left a widower. He devoted himself to theology, and when he came under the King's notice was one of the leading theologians in the University. The story goes that he owed his promotion to a chance conversation with Gardiner, the King's secretary, and Fox, the King's almoner, whom he met at a friend's house in Essex. Talk turned upon the divorce and Cranmer expressed the view that the matter should be regarded as a theological question. Gardiner and Fox reported their conversation to the King, who sent for Cranmer and was so impressed by him that he kept him near him, making him an inmate of the household of Anne Boleyn's father, Sir Thomas Boleyn, recently created Earl of Wiltshire and Ormonde. A new and more hopeful way was opened to Henry. Cranmer was a convinced student of the Scriptures, not as the historical and traditional so much as the living basis and criterion of theological truth. The range of his learning and the vigour of his teaching had given him influence in Cambridge, and now through his efforts theological opinion in the University veered round from a hostile to a friendly view of Henry's case. The divorce was to be found in the divine law, enforced by Scripture, that a man could not marry his brother's wife. Cranmer became essential to the King. He strengthened the royal purpose when it was shaken by the arguments of Henry's brilliant young kinsman, Reginald Pole.[1] He took a wider and firmer view than that of the canonist pleader, Gardiner, and was a more resolute supporter of secular authority. It is curious to think that he came to power through the chance notice of his future rival and that one of his earliest services to the King was the refutation of a young nobleman who, as Cardinal Archbishop of Canterbury, was later to triumph by his death.

In 1530 and 1532 Cranmer was employed as Henry's representative first at Rome and in 1532 at the imperial court. In Germany he made the acquaintance of some of the reformers, including Osiander of Nuremberg, whose niece he married. His marriage was, of course, invalid by the law of the Church to which he still belonged, and in the English Church until 1548. It involved him in much difficulty and opprobrium, and was a private arrangement which is a tribute to the independence of his conscience rather than to his wisdom. It may also be regarded as a proof that he had no expectations of the greatness which was in store for him. On the death of Warham the King passed over Gardiner and all the other bishops in favour of Cranmer. The offer of the archbishopric put him in a difficulty. He did not accept Papal supremacy, yet Henry was not prepared to appoint an archbishop outright against the law of the Church. Such a step would have been most impolitic until the Church of England had been definitely constituted, and yet the King required an archbishop on whom he could rely in order to carry through

---

[1] The only evidence about Pole's views at this time is in a letter from Cranmer to Wiltshire, probably written in 1531; but it seems a fair conjecture that the criticisms of Cranmer were known to and influenced the King.

the change. All that had been done so far had been done within the kingdom and with the consent of Convocation. Parliamentary action had been confined to the Act of Annates, an Act which was permissive and by its own provisions was left to the King as an instrument for negotiation with the Papal Curia during the summer and winter of 1532. England was still in communion with Rome, and its primate had to be canonically elected by the monastic chapter at Canterbury, approved by the Pope, and consecrated with the sanction of Papal bulls and with a sworn promise of obedience to the Papal see. Hence both the Pope and Cranmer had to be managed. The Pope was first asked to believe that the King had done all that he could to resist the importunities of his people in their attack upon the Papal revenues; later he was given to understand that unless the bulls confirming Cranmer's election were issued, the act abolishing annates and first fruits would be enforced. At this time the distance between England and the Papal Court helped Henry rather than the Pope; the bulls were issued at Bologna, 22 February 1533. Henry had secretly married Anne Boleyn in January; the great Act in Restraint of Appeals was debated and passed in February, the bulls arrived in March. Cranmer was consecrated on the 30th, and under his presidency in Convocation the next day the clergy, Bishop Fisher and a few others alone resisting, adopted his view and the verdict of the universities that the King's first marriage was contrary to the Divine law. Shortly afterwards Queen Catherine was declared to be divorced, after a tedious and pedantic process which the new archbishop conducted at the priory of Dunstable.

Cranmer's reluctance to take the oath to the Pope was overcome by the casuistry of a convenient canonist. He might take it under protest. His protestation accordingly may be found entered in his register, with the bulls authorizing his consecration and his oath to Pope Clement VII. The oath, he declared, had no force in so far as it bound him to do anything contrary to the law of God, to the King or his realm, laws and prerogatives, nor did it impede him from taking his share in the reformation of the English Church.[1] This action was never forgiven him. Twenty years later Cardinal Pole set it beside his eucharistic heresies as the most scandalous blot in his heretical life. Whether Cranmer, holding the views which he held and conscious as he was of his ability to forward them, should have withdrawn into private life is a moral issue which could be debated for ever. He made his position perfectly clear. Several months before, the King had called the attention of Parliament to the latent contradiction between the oaths of obedience to the Pope and to himself. In his new role as head of the Church he regarded the bishops as only half his subjects, just as King John had regarded the men who, more than three hundred years before, had wished to do homage to the French king for their Norman lands as well as to remain his men for their English lands. Once Cranmer was consecrated and generally accepted, once Convocation had given the sanction of the clergy to his divorce and second marriage, he could go forward. So in the spring session of the next year, 1534, Parliament gave statutory ratification to all that had been done and pushed it to its logical conclusion. Hitherto the chief instrument had been Convocation.

[1] The most important clause of the oath and the accompanying protestation ran as follows:

The Oath	*The Protestation*
Papatum Romanum et regalia S. Petri adiutor eis ero, ad retinendum et defendendum, salvo meo ordine, contra omnem hominem.	Cum iuramentum . . . praestari . . . me, ante meam consecrationem, aut tempore eiusdem, pro forma potius quam pro esse aut re obligatoria ad illam obtinendam oporteat, non est nec erit meae voluntatis aut intentionis per huiusmodi iuramentum . . . me obligare ad aliquod ratione eorundem posthac dicendum faciendum aut attemptandum quod erit aut esse videbitur contra legem Die, vel contra . . . regem nostrum Angliae, aut rempublicam huius sui regni Angliae, legesve aut praerogativas eiusdem.

Convocation had given the King his title, surrendered its right to independent legislation and, in the name of the Divine law, had withdrawn the matrimonial difficulties of the King from Papal cognizance. But the original impetus was given by the petition of the Commons, a petition which the King had professed to regard as a free and independent expression of the general will. Henceforward Convocation took the second place and the King in Parliament gave a legal character to a national church.

The legislation of 1534 was an application, to all the issues involved, of the political doctrine which was expanded in the famous Act of February 1533 in restraint of appeals. It is known that this Act was not passed without discussion. In the Commons the opposition was inspired mainly by fear of the consequences, but hesitation there was, which Cromwell's arts of management were required to allay. The fear of schism was certainly natural, for the grounds of the Act are found in political history. Recognition is given to the corporate identity of the spiritualty 'now being usually called the English Church' (a curious limitation of the church to the clergy, which reminds us that we are reading Cromwell rather than Cranmer), and the upper house of Convocation is made the final court of appeal in ecclesiastical cases which touch the King. In the beginning of 1533 Convocation had still to express the mind of the clergy on the divorce. But the Act allows no independent standing to the Church, and in the next year Convocation ceased to have any appellate jurisdiction. The clergy are required to fulfil their sacred functions notwithstanding any Papal prohibition. If any spiritual person should refuse to do so, he is liable to a year's imprisonment; if he procures or allocates or abets in any way a Papal mandate he is liable to all the pains and penalties of praemunire. In other words the duty of a priest to adminster the Sacraments was to be a civil as well as a spiritual duty; non-performance was made an offence under an Act of Parliament. It is worth while to set out the historical theory of the preamble of this Act:

Where by divers sundry old authentic histories and chronicles it is manifestly declared and expressed, that this realm of England is an empire, and so hath been accepted in the world, governed by one supreme head and king, having the dignity and royal estate of the imperial crown of the same, unto whom a body politic, compact of all sorts and degrees of people, divided in terms, and by names of spiritualty and temporalty, be bounden and ought to bear, next to God, a natural and humble obedience: he being also institute and furnished, by the goodness and sufferance of Almighty God, with plenary whole and entire power, pre-eminence, authority, prerogative and jurisdiction, to render and yield justice, and final determination to all manner of folk residents or subjects within this his realm, in all causes . . . within the limits thereof, without restraint or provocation to any foreign princes or potentates of the world; the body spiritual whereof having power, when any cause of the law divine happened to come in question, or of spiritual learning, then it was declared, interpreted and showed by that part of the said body politic, called the spirituality, now being usually called the English Church, &c.

The organic theory of the independent State, which I think was very probably taken from Marsiglio of Padua,[1] is given an historical setting. The reformation was to be regarded as a return to the past, a vindication of the rights of the crown against usurped jurisdiction. But there is no suggestion, such as was worked out by later apologists

[1] Cf. *Defensor Pacis*, I. xvii, II. vi. Marsiglio's famous work was first printed at Basel in 1522 and an English translation by William Marshall was published in 1535. Marshall was a protégé of Anne Boleyn's and one of Cromwell's confidential agents. His translations were made under Cromwell's patronage, and it is most unlikely that Cromwell had not studied Marsiglio before the English translation appeared. The *Defensorium Pacis*, as it was styled, appears on the list of prohibited books in 1542 printed in Burnet. The people are said to have greatly murmured at it, and it did not sell. (See Professor Pollard's life of Marshall in the *D.N.B.*)

and theologians, of a primitive independent Church in England. The Church is the clergy, and the function of the church is to declare the divine law; nothing is said of the execution of it. The English Church has not yet succeeded in extricating itself from this conception of its character. In February 1533 it would have been unwise to draw the logical conclusion and to give to the body politic as a whole, in the person of the King, the ultimate voice in the interpretation and execution of the law of God. The Spiritualty was required to declare it a few weeks later in the matter of the King's marriage. But this logical conclusion was foreshadowed in the preamble of the Act, and was not long delayed.

The Papal reply to the proceedings in England in the spring of 1533 was the preparation of bulls of excommunication. Henry in November lodged an appeal which with the statute in restraint of appeals was fastened to every church door in England. The country in 1533 and the following year was put under careful surveillance and royal proclamations, episcopal injunctions, the efforts of preachers enforced the duty of repudiating the bishop of Rome. The centre of activity was parliament in its eventful session during the first three months of 1534. In December 1533 the King's Council had been hard at work. The imperial ambassador reported it met almost daily 'and several learned canonists are summoned to the board'. The result was the carefully worded and drastic legislation which gave statutory definition to all that had been done. The submission of the clergy, the superiority of the Crown to Convocation, the right of the King to nominate bishops for election and, failing election, to appoint by letters patent, the royal ratification of the Act restraining the payment of annates and first-fruits, were all given parliamentary sanction. One important change was made: appeals from the archbishop's courts were to go, not to the upper House of Convocation but to Chancery, and every one had this right of appeal:

Upon every such appeal, a commission shall be directed under the great seal to such persons as shall be named by the King's highness, his heirs or successors, *like as in the case of appeal from the admiral's court*, to hear and definitely determine such appeals, and the causes concerning the same.

Another important Act dealt with dispensations. The Papal power of dispensation, which had developed rapidly since the twelfth century in virtue of the *plenitudo potestates*, had been essential to ecclesiastical administration and to the maintenance of harmonious relations between the various parts of the Church, and between the secular and spiritual powers. It was an ever-springing fount of oil playing upon the ecclesiastical machinery. If a bastard desired to take holy orders, or a clerk to hold more than one benefice with cure of souls, if any particular adjustment in the operation of the canon law were required, the remedy had lain directly or indirectly with the Holy See. The whole controversy regarding the King's divorce had turned first upon the technical procedure and later upon the limitations of the dispensing power. The Act of 1534, which handed over all this jurisdiction to the archbishop of Canterbury, expressed in general terms the distinction recently emphasized by Convocation between human law and the law of God. All human law was subject to dispensation, but dispensation cannot apply to causes (and here Cranmer adopted a more rigid definition than did the canonists) contrary or repugnant to the Holy Scriptures and laws of God. There was no intention to 'decline or vary from the congregation of Christ's Church in any things concerning the very articles of the Catholic faith of Christendom or in any other things declared by Holy Scripture and the Word of God', necessary for salvation. But, with this qualification, dispensation from law within the realm was under the full power and authority of the King and the lords and commons representing the whole State of the realm. There was no law, whatever its origin, not so subject to dispensation. The canon law was not foreign law, but law of foreign origin, accepted, with royal sufferance, by the people as their own. The archbishop was empowered to dispense, not in virtue of any right vested in him as archbishop, but by the King and Parliament. His power extended to such instruments as had previously been obtained from Rome, and if he did not exercise it the King might order the issue of appropriate writs in Chancery. Here we have a clear application of the doctrine of the unity of the State, and of its independence. Here again there is no suggestion of the way in which the sacred law of God could be enforced apart from the secular authority.

Next came the first Act of Succession, the Act under which More and Fisher died. It set the seal of Parliament on the divorce and the rights of the little princess Elizabeth. It declares even more emphatically than the other statutes of the period that no man, of what estate, degree or condition soever he may be, has power to dispense with God's law, and it cites in confirmation the judgement of Convocation, the universities, and the archbishop. The succession was a domestic matter, and certainty was essential; for in the past uncertainty had not only carried confusion, it had also given an opening to the Bishop of Rome, 'contrary to the great and inviolable grants of jurisdiction given by God immediately to emperors, kings, and princes'. More and Fisher would have acquiesced in this Act if it had gone no farther. But the succession involved an oath of obedience; it was the core of the whole revolution, for the rights of the infant princess rested upon the repudiation of all alien jurisdictions. Every subject of full age was to swear to defend to the full extent of his powers the whole effects and contents of the Act.[1] The nation was

---

[1] No definite oath was prescribed in the Act, but a form was devised on the day of the prorogation and incorporated in the second Act of Succession in November. The certificate of the commissioners who administered the oath was made 'as strong and available in the law' as an indictment by a local grand jury.

to form itself, so to speak, into a sworn commune to establish the new settlement. Refusal to take the oath was to be an act of treason.

Although so much had been said about the royal prerogative, Parliament had not yet formally confirmed the position of the King. It crowned its labours in November of this year 1534 by passing the Supremacy Act (26 Henry VIII, c. 1). The title of supreme head on earth, recognized by Convocation in 1530, was enacted by authority of Parliament. Thus the first step in the revolution was also the last, but with three significant differences. The law of the realm rounded off what a declaratory confession of the clergy had begun. The saving clause 'so far as the law of God allows' was omitted. And, in the third place, the scope of the royal power was defined as 'power and authority from time to time to visit, repress, redress, reform, order, correct, restrain and amend all such errors, heresies, abuses, offences, contempts and enormities, whatsoever they be which by any manner spiritual authority or jurisdiction ought or may lawfully be reformed', &c. The King has a spiritual jurisdiction. His Vicar-General could, in virtue of this statement, preside in Convocation. His visitors could supersede episcopal authority, just as in the old days a great eyre superseded all other administration of justice. His injunctions had the validity of ecclesiastical acts. The King in Parliament could define the true faith, so that proceedings in cases of heresy might take place under statutory commissions or even by process of common law in the secular courts, as well as in the ecclesiastical tribunals. In the face of these facts how is it possible to describe the reformation under Henry VIII as the organization of an independent national Church under royal protection? How is it possible to deny that the rejection of Papal authority, far more than the national wars of the later Middle Ages, gave reality to the conception of a united sovereign State, in which the King in Parliament expresses the national will, and this in matters ecclesiastical no less than in civic affairs?

It may be well at this point to examine the considerations which can be urged in modification of these conclusions. The first, and a fundamental, objection might be raised that, as Scripture, in the eyes of the Reformers the main source of the divine law, was so frequently pleaded in justification of the changes in England, a serious limitation was imposed from the outset upon the authority of the King in Parliament. As the Act in restraint of appeals alleged, the spiritualty were the exponents of this divine law, and must have been regarded as possessed of independent authority to expound it. In the words of Bishop Burnet, the King had power 'to oversee and cause that the said Bishops and Priests do execute their pastoral office truly and faithfully, and especially in these points which by Christ and His Apostles were given and committed to them'. This argument is perfectly sound. No one denied that the law of God was far removed above all mundane interference; indeed, in the eyes of the Roman Church, the crime of the schism was increased by the blasphemous assumption that it was inspired by regard for the law of God as well as by regard for English traditions. Also, the right of interpretation was regarded, on theological and historical grounds, as lying in the clergy and not in the laity. The Elizabethan bishops were to find themselves faced by a clamorous regard for the law of God, which Puritans and Separatists declared to be quite inconsistent with the English settlement, and they doubtless resisted the clamour as schismatical no less than as a piece of civil disobedience. On the other hand, it would be hard to find evidence in the sixteenth century, though there is plenty in the seventeenth, that the English Church was regarded as an independent shrine of the divine law, as a society which, in obedience to its own being and responsibilities, had the right to maintain itself against the State. Even Hooker, who did not deny that 'a church as such and a

commonwealth as such are distinguishable things',[1] denied that, as applied to England, there was any force in the
distinction. The very nature of the revolution in Henry
VIII's reign had made a position like this impossible. The
watchwords of conservatives and reformers alike were
unity and obedience. The duty to maintain the law of God
was, so to speak, distributed, or in times of trouble, concentrated in the King. Mistakes might be made, but conscience might be a treacherous guide, and it was better to
endure than to endanger unity. In other words, the attitude at its best was very like the attitude of the great men,
More, Contarini, Pole, and the rest, who regarded the
unity of the Church as the all-important thing, but in
England the unity of the realm took the place of the united
Church in the regard of men. The general view was doubtless less refined. The shadow of *praemunire* lay darkly over
the clergy. The generation which had responsibility in
ecclesiastical affairs after 1532—and changes in the episcopate were numerous in these years—depended upon the
Crown. It wished for nothing less than to be left exposed to
the blasts of public criticism. For it must not be supposed
that the distinction between positive and divine law, so
clear to bishops and canonists, was apparent to or accepted
by all. The great laity had no intention of allowing an independent status to the clerical order. The pains and
penalties of *praemunire* struck at those who exercised jurisdiction contrary to the law of the land, and in the eyes of
lawyers and nobles were an effective safeguard against
prelates who guided a complacent monarch as well as
against those who resisted a strong one. 'Thou art a good
fellow, Bishop,' said Audley the Chancellor to Gardiner,
'look at the Act of Supremacy, and there the King's
doings be restrained to spiritual jurisdiction; and in
another Act it is provided that no spiritual law shall have
place contrary to the Common Law or Act of Parlia-

---

[1] The words are Mr. J. W. Allen's.

ment.[1] And this were not so, you bishops would enter in
with the King, and by means of this supremacy order the
laity as he listed.' Audley did not refer to the law of God
when he spoke of spiritual laws, but in practice episcopal
rule would have been based on the claim to administer as
well as expound divine law, and the nobility would run no
risks. Others went further still at this time. The lawyer
Christopher St. Germain taught that it was for 'the
King's grace and his Parliament' to expound Scripture,
and so decide what the irrefragable law of God is; for the
King with his people have the authority of the Church.
And if they make the Church, then they may expound
Scripture. Indeed, since the Reformation, the sanction of
the law of God has not, in general Anglican opinion, implied any peculiar privilege in the clergy nor any strong
belief in an independent organization of the Church, nor
any unity in the matter among the clergy themselves. In
Henry's reign such views were quite impracticable. Certainly the King did not share them. He regarded himself as
the protector of his creatures, the bishops and clergy, not
as subject to their advice. This is how he spoke to Parliament in 1545:

If you know surely that a bishop or a preacher crieth or
teacheth perverse doctrine, come and declare it to some of our
Council or to us, to whom is committed by God in high
authority to reform and order such causes and behaviour.

'Committed by God.' 'He that judgeth the King judgeth
God,' Tindale had said. There was little danger that this
view would hold in the land of the common law. And the
rights of private conscience were to have a great future in
England. But it is quite clear that for the ordinary man the
distinction between different kinds of law was simply non-
existent. He obeyed the law and believed what he was

[1] The Act confirming the submission of the clergy, 1534 (25 Henry VIII
c. 19). By spiritual law Audley meant constitutions of the clergy. His remark
illustrates very well one of the reasons for giving parliamentary expression to
the submission of Convocation in 1530 and 1532.

told. He was like John Dumbell, the vicar of Southecerney, who when he was asked during Bishop Hooper's Visitation in 1551, to repeat and prove from Scripture the Lord's Prayer, was able to repeat it, and knew it to be the Lord's prayer *propterea quod tradita sit a Domino Rege, ac scripta in libro regio de Communi Oracione*.[1]

These considerations deprive a second argument in favour of the survival of a separately organized Church of most of its force. The spiritualty, commonly known as the Church of England, to use the phraseology of the Act in Restraint of Appeals, had, it can be truly urged, a corporate existence in the provincial convocations which met at the same time as Parliament. There was no breach in the continuity of Convocation; it discussed ecclesiastical problems and granted taxes as of old; its legislation dealt with the doctrine, formularies, law, and discipline of the Church. After a study of the Acts of Convocation, accessible to him, though they were afterwards destroyed in the Great Fire of London, Peter Heylyn the biographer of Archbishop Laud, declared that 'there was but little done in King Henry's time, but that which was acted by the clergy only in their convocation, and so commanded to the people of the King's sole authority'. It may be granted (so the argument would continue) that the activity in Convocation was not so independent and self-directed as the records would make it appear to have been. It was summoned in virtue of the King's writ, it could proceed to no legislative business without the royal licence, it could put none of its decrees into execution without the permission of the King under the great seal. All this is true; but in what respect was Parliament any better off? Have we not here two concurrent assemblies, representative of the spiritualty and laity, expressions of the organic life of Church and State respectively?

There is some force in this argument. Formally, it is an accurate statement of the case. Yet it would be quite mis-

---

[1] *English Historical Review*, xix (1904), 112.

C

leading to describe Convocation as an independent body, or to suggest that it had the life in it which we can see in the Houses of Parliament. As one follows in detail the history of the Reformation from 1534 until the important provincial synod of 1604, and especially until the death of Edward VI, one finds at every step the co-operation of laity and clergy, of royal councillors, lawyers, bishops, and theologians. The guidance of ecclesiastical affairs was a matter of State. An Act of Parliament gave validity to every important change, the Act of the Six Articles in Henry's reign, the two Prayer Books of Edward's reign. The King had the controlling interest in the formulation of articles in the one, the Council in the other reign. The bishops and officers of the Church were in fact the heads and executors of an administrative department of the State. So great was the sense of their inferiority that in 1547 the lower clergy petitioned that, in accordance with ancient practice (a short-lived practice of the fourteenth century), the lower House of Convocation might be adjoined and associated with the lower House of Parliament; or else that statutes concerning religion and causes ecclesiastical might not pass without their sight and assent. They also requested to see the books said to have been prepared by a royal commission in the late reign with regard to the services of the Church. Moreover, during this time Parliament began to give legal sanction to the financial grants of the clergy, which since the middle of the fourteenth century had been an independent act of Convocation. But the most significant obstacle to the freedom of Convocation was the well-known fact that none of its decisions had any legal effect if they were contrary to the common law or Acts of Parliament. In 1620 Coke gave it as his opinion that the royal consent could not give validity to such decisions. We come back to the standpoint of Audley. Convocation was rather 'a collection of individuals deeply interested in the pending measures and well qualified to give advice respecting them, than an authority in any manner co-ordinate with the Crown',[1] or rather, with the King in Parliament.

It is from this point of view that we must consider the curious fact that the English Church has no code of law. Parliament in 1534 allowed continuous validity to the canon law and procedure in so far as it was not abrogated *ipso facto* by the statutes or contrary to the law of the land. Also, authorization was given for the appointment of a mixed commission of thirty-two persons who should have the duty to reduce the surviving law of the medieval Church into a system in harmony with the new settlement. Cranmer worked hard at this task from time to time, but although three statutes of Henry VIII dealt with the appointment of the commission, it was not until the end of Edward VI's reign that the work was done, and then by a smaller commission of eight persons, the archbishop and the bishop of Ely, two theologians (of whom the famous Peter Martyr was one), two civilians, and two common lawyers. Edward died before the *reformatio legum ecclesiasticarum* could be authorized. Archbishop Parker revised the material, and the work was ultimately published by John Foxe, the martyrologist, in 1571, in order to provide information for the House of Commons. But it was refused royal authority. Hence the law of the Church in addition to the statutes and the documents, including the Prayer Book, authorized by statute, consisted of the canons of Convocation, notably those of 1562, and a mass of rules and forms of proceedings which, in the course of time, was gradually worn away to nothing by the encroachments of the secular law. The reluctance of the Crown to give effect to an ordered reformation of the law is very significant, and it is equally worthy of notice that the active interest in it, shown in Elizabeth's reign, came from a Puritan

---

[1] Edward Cardwell, *Synodalia* (Oxford, 1842), p. x. In general, Cardwell's depreciation of the share of Convocation seems to go too far, and is not easily reconciled with his comments elsewhere on the importance of the Canons of 1562 and other transactions in Elizabeth's reign.

section. The Puritans were more concerned with the idea
than with the contents of the book, for they were coming to
feel the necessity of a self-ordered ecclesiastical system free
from the joint management of bishops and privy councillors. But the general character of the Reformation in
Henry's reign and the contemporary concern about the
nature of law suggest considerations of wider interest. The
study and practice of the canon law in the previous centuries had naturally had considerable influence upon the
study and practice of the common law. There was an intimate connexion between the leading principles of law
and theology, and as equitable jurisdiction developed in
England in the Court of Chancery, the experience of the
Church in the application of problems of reason and conscience was of much assistance to those who had to deal
with 'hard cases' in the law. The very fact that the common law was the accepted law in England, powerful
enough at this very time to resist the threatened invasion
of the civil or Roman law, made it all the more important
that the adjustment of the common law to claims of reason
and conscience, whether in the common law courts or in
the courts of equity, should be intelligently provided for.
Hence the well-read lawyer who was interested in the
bearing of legal developments was drawn to the study of
the canon law. He found in the natural law of canonists
and theologians the fundamental principles of all positive
law, he appreciated the value of their experience in the
reasonable construction or interpretation of existing custom, and he saw how equitable remedies depended in the
last resort upon man's natural power 'of discerning between good and evil and of inclining towards the good',
the power which is the sanction of conscience.[1] Now, if
we realize that the thinkers and jurists, who in the six-

---

[1] Vinogradoff, 'Reason and Conscience in Sixteenth-Century Juris-
prudence' (*Collected Papers*, ii. 193–8). This is a study of the most important
work of Christopher St. Germain, the dialogue between a doctor of divinity
and a student of the laws of England.

teenth century were expounding doctrines of the organic unity of the State under the guidance of the Crown, were actively aware of all this medieval experience, we see at once that they would find no difficulty in reconciling the spiritual and secular aspects of society in one united body politic. They were not atheists, they believed in the all-penetrating authority of 'natural law', the rules of reason and conscience, and they could not contemplate the possibility of a fundamental opposition between the law of God, which they could not touch, and the positive law of man. They were medieval enough not to believe in the secular State and modern enough to believe in the self-sufficiency of the State. The great work of Hooker was, in the main, a philosophical statement of their instinctive convictions. What was essential in the canonical system they had got; what was of every day use could be administered in the ecclesiastical courts. But they desired to see no rival to the common law.

The proceedings against heresy are an admirable example of the relations between the canon and the common law in the age of the Reformation. In medieval theory the secular power was the protector, the arm of the Church, and had a particular duty to assist the Church in the extirpation of heresy. The heretic was tried by the Church, but the secular authority was at hand to give aid in his detection and arrest, and had the duty of dealing with an obstinate heretic. In the words of Pope Boniface VIII, the Church handed over the offender for due punishment (*animadversio debita*). From the twelfth century the recognized penalty inflicted upon the obstinate and relapsed heretic was death by fire. In a famous constitution the Emperor Frederick II gave expression to this view, and in another he ordered the secular authorities in his Italian dominions to give aid to the Church; both constitutions were afterwards incorporated in another law which was given universal application throughout the empire and received yet wider authority from the explicit reference made to it by Boniface VIII in the decree already quoted, a decree which was included in the Sect or sixth book of the decretals or codification of the canon law.[1] When, for the first time, heresy became common in England at the end of the fourteenth century, this procedure was adopted. There was some hesitating legislation in the reign of Richard II, but in the next reign (1401) Henry IV issued a writ ordering the execution of Sawtre, a Lollard condemned as a heretic by Convocation. At the same time general effect was given to this procedure by an Act, the famous statute *De heretico comburendo*, which commanded the local sheriff or mayor to receive heretics condemned in an ecclesiastical court, and to burn them publicly in a prominent place. A later act of 1414 (2 Henry V, st. 1, c. 7) emphasized still more the co-operation of the two powers. The royal judges were authorized to make inquiry into heresy; the goods and chattels of the condemned were to go to the King; but again all the judicial proceedings must take place in the ecclesiastical courts. Moreover, it was enacted that the chancellor, treasurer, judges, and all officers of justice must take an oath on appointment to do their utmost to extirpate heresy by assisting the ordinaries and their commissaries. So effect was given to the duty of a prince 'to lay corporal punishment on them which are teachers of perverse things'.[2] It was by virtue of this duty, imposed by oath, that in the early years of King Henry VIII Sir Thomas More as chancellor took cognizance of heresy. He had no power to try heretics, and did not; but he had both the power and the duty to take note of cases which were brought to his attention; and it was for the exercise of this authority, which he used more than once in well-in-

---

[1] Huillard-Bréholles, *Historia diplomatica Friderici secundi*, iv. 5–7, 298–303; v. 201–2; Sexti Decretal., lib. V, tit. ii, c. 18.

[2] Hooker's translation of a phrase quoted by him from the learned Roman Catholic controversialist, Thomas Stapleton (*Laws of Ecclesiastical Polity*, Book VIII, ch. ii. 14, in the Oxford edition of Hooker's *Works*, 1865, ii. 503).

tentioned and sometimes kindly efforts to persuade them of the error of their ways, that he was afterwards accused of being a persecutor of heretics. Again, in virtue of the Acts of Henry IV and Henry V it was the duty of the secular authorities, of executive officers like the sheriffs, to receive and deal with the condemned. It is probable that no additional authority was required and that the officer had no need to await the instruction of any writ.[1]

The acceptance of the royal supremacy brought the trial as well as the execution of heretics under the control of the secular power. In order to give effect to the change, two steps were taken by Henry's Parliament. By an Act of 1534 it was declared that, before any heretic could be executed, the King's writ must be obtained. By an Act of 1539 the King, as supreme head of the Church, was empowered to take action against heresy. At the same time, in the Act of the Six Articles, which was intended to put a stop to diversity of opinion, heresy became a felony against the law of the land. Any man who was convicted of disbelief in the Real Presence in the Sacrament, as defined by the Act, was to be burned as a heretic and suffer full forfeiture as a traitor. The administration of the Act was not left only to the ecclesiastical courts, but was entrusted to commissioners 'for correction of heretics', and these commissioners were to act in accordance with the common law procedure, to receive the presentments of juries and indictments of accusers. This Act had a short life, but it illustrates the change made by the Reformation.

Hence we do not find in Henry VIII's reign, after 1534, that the ecclesiastical courts enjoyed a monopoly in the trial of heresy. The continuity is broken. Convocation no longer declared cases of heresy. We find trials in episcopal courts, trials by special commissioners, attainders by Act

---

[1] Pollard, *Wolsey*, pp. 209–13; and see R. W. Chambers's paper, already mentioned, on More. More's opinion of the necessity of extirpating heresy was, it is hardly necessary to say, quite definite. See his *Dialogue*, Book IV, chapters 13–15, 18.

of Parliament. The sworn national commune, through its various kinds of executive, declares war on heresy, or protects it, or declares it. No longer is it the duty of a sheriff or a mayor to burn a heretic on the strength of an ecclesiastical sentence. He must have the authority of the King. It is important to bear this cumulative evidence in mind when we turn to the proceedings against heresy during the minority of Edward VI, for it has often been said that the two heretics burnt in 1550 and 1551, Joan Bocher and George Parris or Van Paris, were executed by ecclesiastical authority. In the first year of Edward VI the whole of the legislation to which I have referred, from the Acts of Henry IV and Henry V to the Act of Six Articles, was repealed. The object was to allow the free expression of reformed opinion, but the tolerant dispositions of Somerset and Cranmer probably caused the change to be so sweeping. Yet it is clear that there was no idea of going back upon the view that the consent of the secular power was required for the punishment of heresy. The Act of Supremacy and the Act ratifying the submission of the clergy were still law, as they still are. By the one the King had the right to suppress heresy, by the other no ecclesiastical law was in force without royal authority. On 25 May 1547 a certain Dr. Richard Smith made a public recantation of his errors at St. Paul's Cross, in which he affirmed 'that within this realm of England and other the King's dominions, there is no law, decree, ordinance, or constitution ecclesiastical, in force and available by any man's authority, but only by the King's majesty's authority and by parliament'. Moreover, in an amnesty Act passed in 1550 after the rebellions of the previous year, it was enacted that the free pardon 'shall not extend to any person or persons which at any time heretofore have offended in these erroneous opinions hereafter ensuring', and then follows a list of opinions held by the Anabaptists and other persons. The general impression conveyed by these measures and statements is rather that the situation in Henry VIII's reign had made the joint administration of King and conservative bishops too dangerous, than that the State had gone too far in assuming the duty of extirpating heresy. The Act of the Six Articles especially had set a barrier to the tendency of opinion. But nobody wished to allow the growth of the wild and fantastic views, as they were regarded, held by Anabaptists and isolated cranks. They were communistic, anarchical, and depraved. Ecclesiastical proceedings, following the procedure of the old canon law, might properly be adopted against them, provided that they were taken under a royal commission, in virtue of the royal supremacy. Hence Cranmer and others were appointed commissioners *ad hoc* by letters patent to try such persons. Two were burnt, others recanted publicly with faggots in their hands. The unhappy woman Joan Bocher, whom Cranmer had befriended in Henry's reign, and George Parris, who denied the divinity of Christ, were executed after trial by the commissioners, on the instructions of royal writs issued by the King's Council. In short, Protector Somerset, when he took the greatest step yet taken in England in the direction of liberty of religious opinion, did not intend to admit any breach in the unity of the State or of English law. England awoke out of a kind of nightmare, in which King, Parliament, and clergy were struggling. Henceforward the bishops might be left to exercise disciplinary action under the law of the land, by co-operation on royal commissions or in accordance with canonical procedure. In Elizabeth's reign ecclesiastical discipline was mainly in the hands of a commission, although on three occasions in her reign and on two occasions in James I's reign heretics condemned in the ecclesiastical courts were burnt under a royal writ.[1] Legislation about heresy is a very unsafe and

[1] This was the situation in 1401, when Henry IV issued a writ for the burning of Sawtre. The power of the secular ruler was stated in the Act of Supremacy. The penalty of burning, after the repeal of the old legislation in 1547, depended upon no statute, but on the acceptance of it as the customary penalty of common law, based in the end on divine law (see *Rotuli Parlia-*

double-edged weapon. England had enough of it in the reign of Henry VIII and Mary. The discipline in Elizabeth's reign was civil as much as ecclesiastical, against the disobedient rather than against the heretic. The few people who were so perverse as to be outside the social pale might safely be left to the old procedure, and in time the growth of the moral sentiment of toleration made this procedure harmless.

To Catholic and Protestant alike the heretic was one who stood outside the united Church, the Church of the faith, not of institutions. When Cranmer and his colleagues handed Joan Bocher over to the secular arm, they used the old phraseology of the canon law. She was a rotten sheep in the flock, she would not return *ad sanctae matris ecclesiae gremium*.[1] The heretics who suffered in Henry's day included some—Bilney, Frith, Barnes—who would have been safe in Edward's day. The heretics of Edward's day were abhorrent to all. The episcopal injunctions of the 'reforming' bishops of the new learning are hot against them. When the martyr John Bradford was in prison early in Mary's reign he felt moved to write to Cranmer, Ridley, and Latimer, in prison at Oxford, about the new Pelagians of free-willers:

The effects of salvation they so mingle and confound with the cause that if it be not sene to, more hurt will come by them than ever came by the papistes—in so much that their life commendeth them to the world more than the papistes. . . . They utterly contemne all learning.

Indeed, until the middle of the seventeenth century, if we

---

mentorum, iii. 459 a; and Maitland, *Canon Law in England*, pp. 176–8). Maitland seems to me to lay too much stress on the survival of the decrees of Boniface VIII in the canon law still legally operative in England. Apart from the particular penalty, the infliction of which depended on the royal discretion, the exercise of the royal supremacy seems to me to be much more important than the traditional co-operation of the two powers. Both Maitland and Mr. Pollard (*Political History of England*, vi. 71, note) seem to overlook this.

[1] Strype, *Memorials of Cranmer*, iii. 511

except those who died in Henry's reign for their hatred of images and pilgrimages, or for their rejection of the Mass or, as Barnes was, for his theology, heresy as such was an incidental feature in the history of the Reformation. The martyrs who died because they would not accept the supremacy in Henry's reign and repudiate the Pope in Elizabeth's reign suffered under secular law. They were not heretics. Similarly the Puritans and Separatists were not heretics. In one way or another all believed in the one Church, based upon the great dogmas of the faith, whether they insisted on its formal unity, as More and Fisher did, or, with Latimer, confessed

a Catholic church, spread throughout all the world, in the which no man may err, without the which unity of the church no man can be saved; but I know perfectly by God's word [he goes on to say to his judges] that this church is in all the world, and hath not his [sic] foundation in Rome only, as you say.

And so, in Henry's reign and Edward's, the main task was to secure an order for the English Church, part of the Catholic Church, which should ensure its unity in government, institutions, doctrine, and worship. Of the government, enough has been said. It secured the unity of the Church by merging it in the unity of the realm. Of its institutions, a curious mingling of secular and ecclesiastical elements, enough will be said when we come to deal with the reign of Queen Elizabeth. We must now follow the attempts to establish unity in doctrine and worship.

The formal statements were embodied in articles and prayer-book, in a new ordinal, in expositions of doctrine. The methods of enforcement were by visitations, injunctions, and preaching, by the silencing of critics, deprivations, and the promotion to the episcopal bench of those who could be relied upon. The means were commissions, so familiar to students of earlier English history, conferences with ecclesiastics and lawyers, deliberations in convocation. The moving force was always the crown and council, the ultimate sanction always the King in Parliament. There was no systematic advance, for parties were too strong. Projects were framed, discussed, adjourned, or dropped. Now one thing absorbed attention, now another. Yet in the end victory lay with the reformed doctrines. The centre of controversy was the nature of the Sacrament of the Altar or the Lord's table.

The story culminates in two episodes: first the Act of the Six Articles of 1539; secondly, the prayer-books of 1549 and 1552. In all the discussions and during all the changes formal unity was maintained. Bishop Hooper stood out against vestments, and John Knox against kneeling to receive the Sacrament; but both were induced to submit. Gardiner and Bonner accepted the first prayer-book and were powerless to resist the second; but unity was at an end when Edward VI died. The rule of Northumberland and the passing of the second prayer-book and the Articles of Religion would never have won general acceptance. It needed the persecution of Mary's reign and the drastic purging of the episcopate by Elizabeth to restore unity. And by then new causes of dissidence were at work among the Reformers themselves. Foreign influences had made headway. Above all other aids to differences of opinion, the Bible, which in the later years of Henry VIII's reign had been distributed in English in every church, was becoming known to the people, not only through the medium of clerical instruction, but also in the printed vernacular. It was frequently in private use. Hence the conditions of Elizabeth's reign were quite different from those in the earlier period, which we have first to consider.

During the years 1536–9 the issue was fairly joined between the conservative and the forward elements among the clergy. In 1537 the scene of discussion was Convocation, the last occasion on which debate in that assembly seems to have been free and effective. In this year the King and Cromwell had particular reason to go warily and to be guided by the general feeling on matters of doctrine, for in the previous year a serious demonstration had occurred against the dissolution of the monasteries and some new articles of religion. The articles, known as the Ten Articles, had been accepted, rather than debated, by Convocation, and the local exposition of them in every parish was a duty imposed by royal proclamation or injunctions. Special commissioners were appointed to communicate the injunctions to the clergy and to examine and, if necessary, to eject inefficient priests. The storm which arose in the nation made the King pause. The rebels, if they can be called such, had been shocked by the intervention of the secular power in matters affecting the cure of souls and the nature of the sacraments. They had petitioned for a recognition of the unity of the visible church under the Papacy, and the limitation of the royal supremacy to less sacred matters. Gardiner seems to have advised acquiescence and in Mary's reign stated that at this time (1536), as again in 1541, Henry was prepared to 'give over the supremacy again to the Pope, but that he would not seem to do it for fear'. What we do know is that he would not 'approve that counsel that would have us yield to our subjects!' He would take a warning, he would not take instructions. So in 1537 the Ten Articles were quietly displaced by the book entitled *The Instructions of a Christian Man*, circulated by royal authority as the work of the bishops and Convocation. This was the result of the discussions in the Convocation of that year, and it marks a reaction from the policy of the Ten Articles. At the same time there was not the slightest intention to relax the exercise of the royal supremacy nor to limit its range. Bishops and clergy might be used as instruments, more suitable than roving-commissions of the Vicar-General's creation,[1] but the publication of the royal will by injunctions

---

[1] Cranmer saw the importance of this point. He was active in enforcing the injunctions in his own diocese and advised Cromwell to see that other bishops did the same. By which means, he said, 'the evil will of the people

and proclamations continued, and in 1539 Parliament itself was used to give statutory effect to articles of religion. In response to opinion at home and to the necessity of maintaining his reputation for orthodoxy abroad, Henry became more conservative and began to take an even more personal interest in the theological education of his people. The result was the fall of Cromwell and the skilful employment in his service of those incompatible spirits, Cranmer and Gardiner.

In 1537 Cranmer, writing to a foreign reformer, Wolfgang Capito, could say of Cromwell that 'he had himself done more than all others together in whatever had hitherto been effected respecting the reformation of religion and of the clergy', and even while the archbishop was suggesting more episcopal co-operation with the Vicar-General, he required (as Strype says) direction from him in everything. 'So ticklish a thing then was it for the bishops to do any things of themselves without the privity and order of this great vicegerent.' Whatever Cromwell's private opinions may have been, he was pressing at this time for a closer understanding with the German reformers. Anne Boleyn had gone, Jane Seymour died in October 1537 after the birth of the future Edward VI. The new Queen must be of the new persuasion. Cranmer also was at this time in close touch with the continental Reformers. He maintained an independent attitude on most points, but he looked forward to a comprehensive understanding, which might be the basis of anti-Roman union. In the preparation of the Ten Articles of 1536 he and the other bishops who advised the Crown had before them the Confession of Augsburg and the Articles drawn up by Melanchthon at a recent conference at Wittenberg between German theologians and the English ambassadors. Again, in 1538, the ambassadors of the Lutheran princes

---

might be conveyed from the king, and his council, upon the ordinaries, and so the love and obedience of the people both secured to their sovereign.' Strype, *Memorials*, i. 123.

in England had a conference with a royal commission of four prelates and four doctors; Cranmer compiled a list of thirteen articles, based on the Confession of Augsburg, and drafted a revised liturgy which was 'clearly inspired by Bugenhagen's *Pia et vera Catholica et consentiens veteri Ecclesiae ordinatio* (1537), a copy of which had been presented to Henry by the author'[1]. During these critical years Europe was waiting to see how England would declare itself in doctrine and ritual. But Henry was getting tired of these equivocal relations with the subjects of another imperial power. The unlucky marriage with Anne of Cleves hurried on a change of ministers, which the Act of Six Articles had already foreshadowed. Cromwell fell, attainted as a heretic and traitor, and the ex-friar Barnes, one of his chief agents in Germany, fell with him. The executions at the end of July 1540 reveal a fine impartiality. Two days after Cromwell was beheaded as traitor and heretic, Barnes and two colleagues in heresy were burnt, and three Papists were hanged as traitors for decrying the royal supremacy. Luther might well remark, 'What Squire Harry wills must be an article of the faith for Englishmen, for life and death'.

The King, in fact, had not gone very far in a Lutheran direction, and Cranmer was both too English and too circumspect to outrun him in more than desire. Despite the archbishop's studies in Lutheran literature, the Ten Articles, when they appeared, had displeased the Lutherans and aroused the hopes of Reginald Pole. They had disturbed the people by the method of their enforcement and by their omissions rather than by what they actually said. The omission of four out of the seven sacraments aroused most concern, and it was on this question that the conservative bishops, after much debate, succeeded in defeating Cranmer and the other reforming bishops. Cranmer accepted the result in good part and the *Institute of a Christian Man*, or Bishops' Book, went out from

[1] C. H. Smyth, *Cranmer and the Reformation under Edward VI*, p. 35.

Convocation as the reasoned statement of clergy to people of the faith which they should hold. Cromwell's second series of injunctions in 1538 confirmed the injunctions of 1536 and laid down rules for the guidance of the clergy in discipline and preaching and the instruction of their parishioners. They were approved by Gardiner, who was especially pleased by the allusion to the Lenten confession. 'Ha! I see the King's Majesty will not yet leave this auricular confession; methink I smell the King on this point.' And both parties were at one in their insistence upon the royal supremacy. The essential thing was that everything should be done in the King's name and by his authority. Henry's attitude to a General Council, which he expounded in a tract written in 1537, was accepted by the bishops: the right of consent to any oecumenical decrees resided in the head of a sovereign state. Gardiner is believed to have been responsible for a suggestion, made in 1536, that Papal bulls still regarded, through the limited retention of the canon law, as valid in England, should be confirmed in the King's name. Perhaps the most striking illustration is to be found in the Bishops' Book itself. This was debated in Convocation, and issued as the agreed work of the bishops and clergy. The King merely dipped into it here and there at first, but later he studied it more carefully and made suggestions which Cranmer discussed with expressions of the utmost deference. Latimer hoped that, if there was anything 'uncertain or impure in the book, the King would purge away the old leaven'. The prefatory address of the clergy to the King humbly submitted it to his correction, as they had no authority to publish anything without the royal power and licence, although they were all agreed 'that the said treatise was in all points concordant and agreeable to Holy Scripture'.

Yet it should be observed in this place that the treatment in the Bishops' Book of the Sacrament of Holy Orders—a matter on which, as Gardiner rightly remarks, little difficulty was found in coming to an agreement—

opened the way to all the later controversies on the nature of the Church. This part of the book was composed with great restraint and moderation. Much stress is laid upon the point that the spiritual power of priests and bishops is no tyrannical power, but is a moderate power, subject to the limits and ends for which it was appointed by God's ordinance. In a document of this time signed by several bishops, including the Catholic John Stokesley, Bishop of London, we read:

Other places of Scripture declare the Highness and Excellency of Christian Princes Authority and Power; the which of a truth is most high, for he hath Power and Charge generally over all, as well Bishops and Priests as other. The Bishops and Priests have charge of Souls within their own Cures, Power to minister Sacraments, and to teach the Word of God; to the which Word of God Christian Princes knowledge themselves subject; and in case the Bishops be negligent, it is the Christian Princes Office to see them do their Duty.[1]

If the first sentence of this pronouncement is limited by the last, there is nothing here to which a Catholic apologist could object; but it is obvious that two opposed trains of reasoning could be followed from the passage and, still more, from the exposition in the Bishops' Book. The one, as we shall see, was followed by Cranmer. The other emphasized the divine sanction given to the authority of the ministers of the Church, made episcopal government a mark of the Church, and claimed that any society which was part of the Church militant on earth must be organized, on its spiritual side, under a continuous hierarchy. This is the position of Hooker, and it is not inconsistent with the conception of identity of Church and State, organized as one whole under the King in Parliament. It says that, in virtue of the general acceptance of the divine law, found in Scripture, as the basis of social order, the

[1] Printed by Burnet in his collection of records added to Book III, No. x.

State must be spiritually guided or governed in a particular way. But the next step in the argument was easy, namely that this government in accordance with the law of God had a separate validity in itself apart from the State, that the Church of England is a moral if not a legal corporation, an expression, apart from the secular order, of the universal Church, that the bishops are much more than isolated officials who can trace their authority back to the Apostles. There is no evidence that such views had any weight in Tudor England, but the door to them was never closed. In Henry VIII's reign, when the difficulty lay rather in the maintenance than in the destruction of continuity, and episcopal authority was of practical necessity for securing order and unity, and yet was an object of everyday criticism from all sides, nobody saw the slightest justification for closing it.

The object of the Ten Articles, and of the *Institutes of a Christian Man* or the Bishops' Book, as it was the object of all the definitions of the age, was the attainment of peace and unity. When Cromwell, as the King's vicegerent in Convocation, opened the proceedings of Convocation in 1537, he declared that 'the King studieth day and night to set a quietness in the Church, and he cannot rest until all such controversies be finally debated and ended through the determination of you, and of the whole Parliament'. The Bishops' Book and the royal injunctions did not still controversy. At the end of 1538 the King had to summon the justices of the peace to his aid. They had been very helpful in putting down the supporters of the Pope; they must now detect and punish the seditious people who misrepresented the injunctions and the 'cankered persons' who so read them as to be unintelligible. Some people, Henry complained, actually set it about that the injunction for the keeping of church registers was a prelude to the taxation of christenings, weddings, and burials, and that the rigorous extirpation of the cult of St. Thomas Becket was a step to the abolition of the liberties of the realm for which the saint had died.[1] The instructions to the justices came between two general proclamations against disputes and disorder among the people, defining which ceremonies could still be used in church, and enjoining the bishops and clergy to instruct the people every Sunday on their 'right use and effect'. Finally, Parliament came to the rescue. At last there would be 'thorough unity and uniformity'. After a committee of bishops had failed to come to agreement, the laity, led by the Duke of Norfolk, took the business in hand, and in spite of lengthy objections raised by Cranmer and five other bishops, the Act of the Six Articles was passed. The conservatives had won, and they had won through king and laity. The orthodoxy of England was grounded in the royal supremacy and Parliament. The people, wrote the French ambassador, showed great joy. An unknown lord wrote:

And also news here, I assure you never prince shewed himself so wise a man, so well learned, and so catholic, as the king hath done in this parliament. With my pen I cannot express his marvellous goodness, which is come to such effect, that we shall have an act of parliament so spiritual, that I think none shall dare say, in the blessed sacrament of the altar doth remain either bread or wine after the consecration: nor that a priest may have a wife: nor that it is necessary to receive our Maker 'sub utraque specie'; nor that private masses should not be used as they have been: nor that it is not necessary to have auricular confession.[2]

The Act did not imply reaction; rather it was a definition of heresy in matters which were under dispute. The bishops as a whole believed in the real presence, though

[1] The injunctions of 1538 ordered *inter alia* the keeping of registers and also the abolition of any commemoration of St. Thomas Becket. Becket had long been the symbol of the old order in popular controversies. In the course of his trial in Edward VI's reign Bishop Bonner was described by Sir Thomas Smith as wishing to be another Becket. The fear that supremacy might turn to absolutism is significant.

[2] *Memorials of Cranmer*, i. 415–16.

they might differ about the interpretation of it. Communion in both kinds had never been allowed and auricular confession had never been forbidden. Many clergy had married, but celibacy was still the law of the Church. It was intended to put a stop to all further disputes on these issues, and to make heresy about them part of the criminal law, administered by the royal justices as well as by the ecclesiastical courts. The Act had a political as well as a religious origin and was not strenuously enforced until four years later. Latimer and Shaxton, the bishop of Salisbury, resigned their bishoprics, and Gardiner displaced Cranmer in the royal counsels. Then, in 1543, persecution was more active. Gardiner had helped to bring about an Anglo-imperial alliance and, as ambassador in Germany in the previous year, had argued with Lutheran divines and had secret, but authorized, negotiations with the Pope. In 1543, largely through his influence, the Bishops' Book was succeeded by the King's Book, *A Necessary Doctrine and Erudition for any Christian Man*, in which the sacraments were discussed more fully and, to Cranmer's chagrin, the tone was more orthodox. The royal share in it was greater than in the Bishops' Book, and during the rest of his reign Henry did not modify his position. One thing he would not do: he would never surrender his own judgement. At one time, his last Queen, Catherine Parr, was in serious danger from her dallying with heresy, and her enemies expected her fall, but Henry was placated by a humble and graceful submission. At another time, everybody was expecting the fall of Cranmer, whose diocese and cathedral were by no means so united as the conservatives would have wished. Cranmer had urged more drastic action against images, and seized any opportunity to press his views on the King. He had appointed six preachers, three of the old, three of the new learning, to be with him and to preach at Canterbury. He was known to be at heart opposed to the trend of events since 1536, the year of Cromwell's rule and the publication of the Ten Articles. Conspiracy against him came to a head and a commission to inquire into the state of affairs in his diocese was appointed. But Henry made him its president and refused to listen to charges against him. In his will he included Cranmer, as he could hardly fail to include him, in the council of regency to be about his young son; and he omitted the name of Gardiner. He is reported to have observed that, while he could manage the bishop of Winchester, nobody else could. The rightful protectors of Jane Seymour's son were Jane Seymour's brothers and friends, with wise men of both parties who, it might be hoped, would work together. He seems to have felt that unity was more important than the safeguarding of orthodoxy. As he said, in the case of Cranmer: 'There remaineth malice among you, one to another, let it be avoided out of hand, I would advise you.'

Indeed, he had no reason to congratulate himself on the success of his policy. The end of controversy promised in 1539 was not in sight. It went on in secret under the dark and terrible shadow of the law. The policy of the ecclesiastical régime in Henry's last years is set out in the admirable injunctions issued in 1542 by the far from admirable Bonner, who had succeeded Stokesley as bishop of London (1540). The clergy were to be orderly and temperate, to have their garb decent and distinctive, to read the Scriptures chapter by chapter every day, to preach simply and without any controversy, expounding the Gospel or Epistle for the day, to leave to properly authorized preachers any discussion of problems of the faith, 'the rehearsal of any opinion not allowed, for intent to reprove the same'. But we get a very different picture from the records of these years. The result was described by the King himself, in the famous speech, preserved in Hall's chronicle, which he made to Parliament on Christmas Eve 1545:

I see and hear daily that you of the Clergy preach one against another, teach one contrary to another, inveigh one against

another, without charity or discretion. Some be too stiff in
their old mumpsimus, others be too busy and curious in their
new sumpsimus. Thus all men always be in variety and discord and few or none preach truly and sincerely the word of
God, according as they ought to do.

Then, turning to the laity, he rebuked their railing of
bishops and slandering of priests, and, in words already
quoted, reminded them that it was his business to reprove
the teachers of error. They were no judges of such high
matters. And, he went on:

Although you be permitted to read Holy Scripture, and to
hear the word of God in your mother tongue, you must understand that it is licensed you so to do only to inform your own
consciences, and to instruct your children and family, and not
to dispute and to make Scripture a railing and a taunting stock
against priests and preachers, as many light persons do. I am
very sorry to know and hear how unreverently that most
precious jewel the Word of God is disputed, rhymed, sung and
jangled in every ale-house and tavern, contrary to the true
meaning and doctrine of the same.

Here, in the King's words, we come to the chief occasion of
strife. It is one of the most curious facts in the history of the
Reformation, that in the very years when the most drastic
law of its kind in the history of England was on the statute
book, to enforce rigidity and uniformity of doctrine, the
Scriptures had been officially spread broadcast through
the land in the English tongue.

The use of the Scriptures as the authority which justified most of the great changes in England, and the fervent
interest in Biblical study shown by Cranmer and the reforming party in the Church had made the publication of
the English Bible under official sanction simply a question
of time, and the limitations upon its circulation a matter of
expediency. Further, the revival of Biblical study was part
of what is sometimes termed the Christian renaissance as a
whole. It influenced Catholic humanism everywhere. Sir
Thomas More, for example, repudiated the charge that

the bishops were hostile to an English Bible as such, if it were purged of the errors of Wycliff and Tindale, and issued without tendencious comment and prefaces. His own view was unequivocal. He had never heard any reason why the Bible should not be translated, and for his part he would not 'withhold the profit that one good devout un-learned layman might take by the reading, not for the harm that a hundred heretics would fall in their own wilful abusion'. It was the duty of ordinaries to take great care about the text and to exercise discretion in allowing its use, just as a father appoints 'which of his children may for his sadness keep a knife to cut his meat, and which shall for his wantonness have his knife taken from him for cutting of his fingers'. More was profoundly convinced that heresy did not come from the common men, but from spiritual and intellectual pride:

Seldom hath it been seen that any sect of heretics hath begun of such unlearned folk as nothing could else be [i.e. knew nothing but] the language in which they read the scripture; but there hath always commonly these sects sprungen of the pride of such folk as had, with the knowledge of that tongue, some high persuasion in themself of their own learning beside.

In a rather more timid spirit very much the same view was taken, after very free and open conference, by an assembly of prelates and divines which the King had called together in May 1530. The occasion of this con-ference was the dangerous spread of heretical books, mainly written or printed abroad. Warham, the arch-bishop, circulated an account of the proceedings. After in-structing preachers to denounce the pernicious writings of the new learning, he describes a discussion which had taken place during the conference on the advantage and disadvantages of an English Bible. The general opinion was definitely against an authorized translation at that time, but the King declared his intention of having the New Testament faithfully and freely translated by learned men, so that it might be issued at a more convenient season. In the epoch-making year 1534 the upper House of Convocation authorized Cranmer, the new archbishop, to petition the King on the same two points: the extirpation of pernicious books and the translation of the Bible, also on the prohibition, under penalty, of disputations by the laity on matters of faith and on the Scriptures. These matters are always found together: the desire to give access to the Scriptures, and the concern with popular disputes on religious things.

It is not necessary to repeat here the well-known story of the English Bible, how the bishops proceeded some way with a joint revision of an old English translation,[1] how the late Austin Friar, Miles Coverdale, completing the labours of Tindale, printed at Zürich the first entire translation, and how an official Bible, based mainly upon Coverdale's work, was authorized for distribution in the churches by the injunctions of Cromwell (1538). A whole Bible of the largest volume was to be set up in a convenient place in every church, the charges to be divided between the parson and the parishioners. There was to be no altercation or contention, but there was also to be no discouragement from the reading or hearing of the said Bible. Naturally enough, the response to this command was slow; it is clear from a proclamation of May 1541 that many parishes had neglected to act upon it. But the great change was made and the Scriptures in the vernacular, with Cranmer's noble preface (1540), could be read by all who wished.

These arrangements were not so impressive as they sound. In most parts of the country, we may well imagine, things went on very much as they had always done. The village parishioners would make little of the Ten Articles and the Injunctions which were often read to them in a slipshod or perfunctory way. They would not hear of the Bishops' Book and the King's Book. As Gardiner satirically

[1] Gardiner had translated the Gospels of St. Luke and St. John. It is erroneous to suppose that he was opposed to an English Bible as such.

pointed out, when the Book of Homilies was circulated in Edward's reign, there was much less desire to hear sermons, either in town or country, than Cranmer seemed to suppose, and a good thing too. There was a lot of unnecessary fuss and the people were quite indifferent.

So with the Bible. We must not suppose that there was a general rush to hear or desire to read. It would lie solitary in the church in most places. On the other hand, efforts were made during these years to bring home to the people the meaning of the faith and the solemnity of the sacraments. (We know from Hooper's visitation of his diocese in 1551 how appallingly ignorant all the clergy were, how unfitted to obey the episcopal injunctions to preach and teach.) Cranmer enjoined his clergy in 1538 to admit no young men or women to their first Communion until they had recited openly in church the *Pater Noster*, the Creed, and the Ten Commandments in the vulgar tongue. And we know that in some places the presence of the large Bible encouraged persons who could read and had the courage or the vanity or the evangelical desire, as the case might be, to improve the occasion, to gather people about them. Some read only, others ventured to expound. The conservatives became alarmed. They had not approved the translation as such. Gardiner, for example, objected to the attempt to give English equivalents of the numerous words, *ecclesia*, *sacramentum*, *religio*, and the like, which in Latin, as interpreted by the age-long wisdom of the Church, had a special significance. Convocation in 1542 got the royal consent to a revision of the new Bible, but the King afterwards, to the resentment of most of the bishops, transferred the matter to the universities, which did nothing. The bishops significantly protested that the 'Universities were much decayed of late, wherein all things were carried by young men, whose judgements were not to be relied on, so that the learning of the land was chiefly in this Convocation.' But this was one of the points in which the King showed his common sense. If in that heated atmosphere the translation of the Scriptures were to be made a matter of detailed theological controversy, there would be no end. In the next year, however, Parliament dealt with the scandal in an Act 'for the advancement of true Religion and for the abolishment of the contrary'. The people who presumed to read, teach, or preach the Scriptures openly in church, without authority, were made liable to a month's imprisonment. Persons who printed, sold, or kept unauthorized translations of the Scriptures were made liable to heavy fines. No person under the degree of yeoman might possess the authorized translation to read to himself. No woman at all, if she were not a noblewoman or gentlewoman, might read it. This absurd Act at any rate suggests that a large number of people were reading it. If the policy implied in the Act of the Six Articles was to prevail, the Bible ought never to have been circulated at all; for the general situation at home and abroad was quite different from that which existed even in Sir Thomas More's time, some fifteen years earlier.

The Council of the boy King Edward adopted the same policy, but in a different spirit and with a very different end in view. It did not define heresy by Act of Parliament: the statutes against heresy, including the Act of the Six Articles, were swept away. As we have seen, nobody in Edward's reign was dealt with as a heretic, except those, repudiated by both parties, who had come under the influence of the Anabaptist and similar movements. The Protector's attitude was twofold: he did not believe, and he did not wish to believe, in the possibility of repressing those who believed in innovation; and he preferred to impose uniformity, as a matter of public order, by even more systematic exercise of the secular authority. Parliament and commissions of Council were the active agents of change, as in Henry's reign, and Convocation was more impotent. The bishops were the advisers of the Crown, and Cranmer is the outstanding figure of the reign; but the co-operation of the episcopal bench and clergy as a whole with the secular authority was not possible, while the conservatives were still so numerous and influential. Cranmer preferred to work with committees and in consultation with the foreign divines who play so large a part in the theological deliberations of this period. Gardiner and Bonner, the leaders of the Catholic party, were deprived for disobedience, not of course for heresy, just as a parson who refused to obey episcopal injunctions might be deprived. Such, in general, were the circumstances under which the Act of Uniformity was passed in 1549, and the first Prayer Book in the English tongue displaced the service books of the Middle Ages.

A lengthy correspondence between Gardiner on the one part and the Protector, Sir William Paget, and Cranmer on the other, enables us to understand the attitude of the conservatives and the significance of innovations in the first year or so of Edward's reign. The Council had decided that, as bishops exercised 'authority of spiritual jurisdiction' by virtue of the royal licence, their commissions ought to be renewed in the new reign. The new licence stated that it was the duty of the bishop to acknowledge his dependence upon the Crown for the exercise of his functions and his obligation to surrender them when required. Gardiner, protesting to Paget against the use of the word 'delegate', which appeared in his new commission, seems to have objected not to the view that he owed his commission to the King, but to the implication that his authority depended only upon the Crown and therefore that he might run the risk of exceeding it, so incurring the penalties of praemunire. 'I have been exercised', he wrote, 'on making of treaties.' He knew the importance of words and phrases. 'It would be a marvellous matter if, after my long service and the loss of my master, I should lose that he gave me by construction of a commission.' The argument would seem to be that, quite apart from the theological issue as to the nature and origin of episcopal authority, a bishop must be regarded as possessed of a standing by common law. He was an ordinary, not a delegate appointed for a particular purpose. This was a return, though not on the same ground, to the position which Gardiner had taken up in defence of Convocation in 1532. Paget and his colleagues, on the other hand, had no hesitation in maintaining that, if a reformation were desired, the government must expect its ministers, secular or ecclesiastical, to be pliable in executing it. Hence they brushed aside all the legal objections raised later by Gardiner and Bonner to the process, which led to the bishops' deprivation. The bishops had a definite commission from the King; they refused to execute it, or at the least quibbled and equivocated. It was not for them to argue about their legal rights as bishops. If a spell of confinement in the Fleet or the Tower did not bring them to reason, they must be dismissed, just as any other state official could be dismissed. When Bonner threatened to appeal, Sir Thomas Smith, one of the committee of council appointed to deal with him, asked to whom he *could* appeal? He could not appeal to the Pope, and if he appealed to the King and Council, he was appealing to the body which was actually trying him. A plea of unlawful dismissal could not lie against the Crown. This was the way in which Elizabeth dealt with the bishops at the beginning of *her* reign. After the fall of Somerset, the bishops in the House of Lords strove to regularize their position. Their authority, they said, was despised by the people and their jurisdiction annulled by proclamations.[1] But, though they were invited to draw up a Bill, nothing definite was done.

In the face of this attitude Gardiner could not hope to stem the tide of innovation. He argued that King Henry's settlement was wise and should be regarded as fixed, until the King came of age. So great was his admiration for it that he wrote of it almost as though it should be treated as

---

[1] Gardiner, iii. 172

a fundamental thing, part of the common law of the land.

Though some would say that he [Henry VIII] had in know-ledge but one eye and saw not perfectly God's truth, yet for us it were better to go to heaven with one eye after him, than to travail here for another eye with danger to lose both. . . . If the wall of authority which I accounted established is once broken, and new water let in at a little gap, the vehemency of novelty will flow farther than your Grace would admit.

So he wrote to Cranmer about the Book of Homilies; and earlier in this year 1547 he wrote to Somerset about a scheme of reform laid down by Barlow, bishop of St. David's, in one of his sermons:

If my Lord of St. David's or such others have their head cumbered with any new platform, I would wish they were commanded, between this and the King's Majesty's full age, to draw the plot diligently, to hew the stones, dig the sand and chop the chalk in the unseasonable time of building; and when the King's Majesty cometh to full age to present their labours to him; and in the meantime not to disturb the state of the realm. . . . In quiet ye be strong, in trouble ye be greatly weak.

Somerset did not read the facts like this. He sympathized with the innovations and regarded England as one of the reformed countries; and he entirely refused to agree that Henry VIII had left matters in a satisfactory condition. There was doubt and disorder everywhere in opinion, and a new effort must be made to secure uniformity. This is the burden of the preamble to the Act of Uniformity in 1549, and of a letter to the Princess Mary in July. The princess had urged that her father had secured godly order and quietness with general consent. Somerset marvelled at this interpretation of the past and proceeds:

Then was it not that all the spiritualty nor yet the temporalty did so fully assent to his godly orders as your Grace writeth of. Did not his Grace also depart from this life before he had fully finished such godly orders as he minded to have established to all his people if death had not prevented him? Is it not most true that no kind of religion was perfited at his death but left all uncertain, most like to have brought us in parties and divisions if God had not only helped us? And doth your Grace think it convenient it should so remain? God forbid.

It is not necessary to describe at length the new effort after Uniformity. To these years (1547-53) we owe the Prayer Book, the Ordinal, the Articles; at this time the right of the clergy to marry was acknowledged by Convocation and ratified by Parliament. The innumerable chantries were abolished, and a crusade undertaken against images, crucifixes, and so-called idolatry of all kinds. The teachings of the bishops and clergy became increasingly Protestant, and the Sacrifice of the Altar became the communion in both kinds. And disturbance grew, just as it had grown after the previous settlement of 1534-9. Something must be said of the way in which these things were done, and by whom they were done, and of the effect of them upon the temper of the people.

In all that was done the initiative was taken by the Protector and his colleagues in the Council of regency. The important changes were debated in Parliament and were given the authority of Parliament. Convocation might or might not be invited to co-operate. In form, therefore, we see little change of procedure in the reign of Edward VI. But the conditions were in reality very different. Hitherto the personality of the King had been dominant everywhere, now the leaders in policy were men who worked increasingly under the influence of party. In order to justify himself in the face of Gardiner's criticisms the Protector had to procure the repeal of the Act which 'would have enabled the King, when he attained the age of twenty-four to annul all Acts of Parliament passed in his minority simply by letters patent'. Similarly, the repeal of the Act of the Six Articles was necessary before Cranmer and the bishops could safely discuss the theological questions relating to the Mass. Gardiner argued with much truth that the new Government, by refusing to mark time during the period of the royal minority, was in fact guilty of a breach of trust. It was not leading a united people with due respect for the constitutional ideas implied in the rule of King in Parliament, but was dragging the people in the wake of a party. In Gardiner's view the new policy of uniformity in preaching, liturgical order, and discipline was a tyrannical interference with a traditional system which was in itself good and would continue to work well if the government would maintain order and keep the balance even. He thought that the general visitation of the kingdom and the enforcement of injunctions issued by the council were illegal, and he detested the new book of homilies issued in the first months of the new reign. His criticism led to his first detention, just as his balanced survey of the general position and his adherence to the old theology led later to his long imprisonment. He wished the people to be left alone: 'Truth', he wrote to Cranmer, 'is able to maintain itself and needeth no help of untrue allegations.'

Although there was much wisdom in Gardiner's view, he undoubtedly failed to realize, indeed he could not have realized, that only Henry VIII himself could have done what he desired the Protector to do. As we have seen, the picture of peace and unity drawn by Gardiner was very far from the facts even in the late king's reign. The Protector would have found it hard to stand still, even if he had wished. In any case his personal inclinations led him to co-operate with Cranmer in seeking a solution for the burning question of the day, the controversy about the Sacrament of the Altar. England was involved in the issue which had rent the Protestants of Germany asunder, and was now regarded as the essential issue between the more advanced reformers and the Roman Church. In the letters and controversial writings of these years we find little concern with the nature of the Church. The new men around Cranmer, whether Englishmen or foreigners, were not disturbed by this problem, as were the refugees who came back to England after Mary's reign ten or twelve years later. Nor does it seem to have troubled the conservative bishops, men like Tunstall of Durham and Thirlby, the bishop of the new and temporary see of Westminster, nor Gardiner himself, provided that the policy of Henry VIII was respected. The reforming element looked to the King and council as a matter of course. Hooper, the former Cistercian monk, who came back to England from exile in the spring of 1549 with ideas far more definitely fixed than those of most of his English friends, and with a rigid conscience which was shortly to involve him and the government in trouble, saw in the young king and his advisers the way of salvation:

O how great shall the King's Majesty and the Council's reward be for their thus doing! They shall triumph for ever with God in such joys as never can be expressed with tongue or pen, without end in heaven, with David, Ezechias, and Josijahu.

And the natural functions of council and Parliament, as the exponents of the truth, are taken for granted in the letter sent by Edward VI to the archbishop on Christmas Day 1549. Referring to the new Prayer Book he said, or was made to say:

We therefore by the advice of the body and state of our Privy Council, not only considering the said Book to be our act, and the act of the whole state of our realm assembled together in Parliament, but also the same to be grounded upon Holy Scripture, agreeable to the order of the primitive Church, &c.

There is not a word about ecclesiastical organization, and in fact it is now generally agreed that the first Prayer Book of Edward VI was not even submitted to Convocation. One of the very earliest reports which have survived of a the debate in Parliament is of a disputation between the bishops in the House of Lords in December 1548, when the Lord Protector, 'because it seemed most necessary to the purpose, willed them to dispute whether bread be in the sacrament after the consecration or not'.[1] And, when the Prayer Book was debated and divided upon in the following year, the proceedings took place in Parliament.

To what extent the eucharistic controversy affected the country as a whole it would be hard to say. As subsequent events were to show, change was regarded with indifference or hostility in many parts of England. The clergy of Oxfordshire refused to use the new Prayer Book and many of them suffered death as rebels in the tumults of the time; the clergy in the west were able to rouse the peasants in what for a time seemed likely to be a formidable rebellion. On the other hand, the 'new learning' had widespread effect in the towns, especially in London, and in the University of Cambridge. The new government did not create, but was faced by, the agitation which the new policy was designed to soothe. The first Act of Parliament of the reign was directed against those who spoke irreverently of the sacrament of the altar, and it is clear that, under the influence of reforming preachers, the eucharist was frequently at this time the subject of popular discussion, which sometimes took the form of, or was merged in, anti-clerical violence. Pamphleteers indulged in a freedom of speech whose blasphemy was rarely, if ever, equalled in the long history of English pamphlet warfare. To this time belong the descriptions of the Mass as 'Jack-in-the-box', 'Round-robin', 'the poetical changeling', and the corruption of the solemn words of consecration *Hoc est corpus* into Hocus-pocus. Such was the setting in which Cranmer and his friends set to work to devise a settlement which should be positive as well as repressive, English rather than Latin, comprehending as much as possible of the old in a reforming tendency. The archbishop had long wished for this opportunity, and now it had come. For ten years, so far as he could, he had worked at the task. He was not a revolutionary, coming to a fresh task, but the

[1] Printed in Gasquet and Bishop, *Edward VI and the Book of Common Prayer* (1890), pp. 397–443, from Royal MS. 17 B. XXXIX.

D

primate whose learning and experience had been steadily directed by, and had intensified, his purpose. Since 1538 he had worked upon ritualistic measures, some of which still survive. Since 1546, under the influence of Ridley, he had passed from his belief in the real presence, which he had regarded as a catholic doctrine to be accepted, while the Roman dogma of transubstantiation was to be rejected, to that difficult view which his opponents, like many modern theologians, found it so hard to distinguish from Zwinglianism.[1] He was in consequence more at liberty to turn for aid to the foreign reformers who, generally at his invitation, came to England at this time— the gentle Spaniard, Dryander, learned in the Mozarabic rite; the cultivated Italian, Peter Martyr, once the friend of reforming Papalists; the learned Martin Bucer, who had for so long tried to bridge the gulf between the Protestant parties in Germany and Switzerland. A project very dear to Cranmer in these years was the union of the continental and English reformers in a common understanding. But he was always the primate, the English theologian deeply read in the Fathers and in liturgical history, seeking a settlement suited to English needs. He never forgot that he was a statesman, a member of the council, acting with theologians and canonists and laymen under the informal commission given to him by the King and the Protector. His independence and deliberateness for a time maddened the ardent reformers, the English and foreign correspondents of Calvin and Bullinger, who watched each act of his, and treasured with eager anticipation every utterance. The conferences at Windsor and Chertsey, in which the future measures were discussed and prepared for council and Parliament, were in 1548 and 1549 the centre of the reforming movement in England.

---

[1] The fullest attempt to explain Cranmer's theology of the sacrament is in C. H. Smyth, *Cranmer and the Reformation under Edward VI* (Cambridge, 1926). Mr. Smyth's definition of it as Suvermerianism appears to rest upon a misconception of the meaning of this word.

The first change, though welcomed by the Protestants, was not inconsistent with medieval and Roman doctrine. It was embodied in the Act against revilers, already mentioned, and in the 'Order for the Communion', issued on 8 March 1548 by royal proclamation and made compulsory upon the clergy by an ordinance of 13 March. The Act, which was submitted to Convocation before it was passed by Parliament, directed that the faithful should receive the communion in both kinds, as well as providing that after 1 May revilers of the sacrament should be presented by local juries before the justices of the peace in the presence of the bishop or his deputy. The 'Order for the Communion' is a brief pamphlet setting out, in the English tongue, a short service for the communion of the laity. It consists of exhortations to communion and the words of administration, and was afterwards incorporated in the Prayer Book. It is of Lutheran origin, for the *Pia consultatio* of Hermann of Wied, archbishop of Cologne (1543), upon which it is based, was due in the main to Martin Bucer, and had passed through the hands of Melanchthon. But neither in the Act of Parliament, which directed that communion should be received in both kinds, nor in the Order which prescribed the ritual, was there anything distinctly Protestant. The priest still made his communion in Latin according to the Sarum use. Communion in both kinds, which was generally recognized to have been the usage of the primitive Church and which was papally recognized in Catholic Germany in 1564, was not heretical, while the Act, by explicitly 'not condemning the usage of any Church out of the King's Majesty's dominions', would seem to suggest that the new order was not to be regarded as theologically necessary. In 1548 and, indeed, in 1549 Cranmer and his colleagues carefully refrained from making the ritual and prayers of the Church capable of expressing only, and nothing more nor less than, his increasingly definite standpoint in regard to the eucharist. He was more than a theologian learned in all the liturgies of the past, he was a priest who for thirty years had, in celebrating the sacrament, used words and prayed prayers which had become part of his spiritual life. The language of the Order for the Communion and of the Prayer Book grew out of his religious experience; it was much more than the literary expression of his theological learning. Even the changes made in the second Prayer Book of Edward VI are regarded in some theological quarters as capable of a wider interpretation. But I am not competent, and am not here called upon, to express any opinion in this difficult controversy.

The first Prayer Book, which followed a month after the Orders for the Communion, was the next step in a Protestant direction. It was prepared by a commission and seems to have been submitted by the Council to a 'synod of bishops', to use Bucer's phrase, in October 1548. With the exception of Day, bishop of Chichester, all the bishops accepted the book, but several, of whom Thirlby was the chief, agreed to it in general for the sake of unity, while reserving some points, notably the omission of the elevation of the host, in the hope that full agreement would be reached later. The book next came before Parliament. In a very interesting letter to Bucer, who had not yet come to England, Peter Martyr gave his impressions of the recent debate. He wrote from Oxford on 28 December:

The other matter which distresses me not a little is this, that there is so much contention among our people about the eucharist, that every corner is full of it. And even in the supreme council of the state, in which matters relating to religion are daily brought forward, there is so much disputing of the bishops among themselves and with others, as I think was never heard before. Whence those who are in the lower house, as it is called, go up every day into the higher court of parliament, not indeed for the purpose of voting, (for that they do in the lower house), but only that they may be able to hear these sharp and fervent disputations. Hitherto the popish party has been defeated, and the palm rests with our friends, but especially with the Archbishop of Canterbury, whom they till now were wont to traduce as a man ignorant of theology, and as being only conversant with making of government; but now, believe me, he has shewn himself so mighty a theologian against them as they would rather not have proof of, and they are compelled against their inclination to acknowledge his learning and power and dexterity in debate. Transubstantiation, I think, is now exploded, and the difficulty respecting the presence is at this time the most prominent point of dispute; but the parties engage with so much vehemence and energy as to occasion very great doubt as to the result: for the victory has hitherto been fluctuating between them.

The report which survives of this debate shows that with the exception of the Protector and the Earl of Warwick (the later Duke of Northumberland) the bishops were the disputants in the crowded assembly. Some concessions were made, notably the substitution of the words *flesh* and *blood* for *bread* and *wine*. Bonner had insisted that the doctrine implied in the latter was not decent, 'because it hath been condemned abroad as an heresy; and in this Realm: example of Lambert'. But the conservatives were voted down on the book as a whole when it came to the final vote on the Act of Uniformity, by which it was authorized (21 January 1549). The critical debates had been upon the eucharist, but the Prayer Book, it is unnecessary to say, comprised a revised breviary and orders for all the rites and ceremonies of the Church as well as the order for the Communion. It was part of a plan for uniformity, and displaced all the old service books. Drawings upon the Use of Sarum and many other liturgies, old and new, it provided for the Church of England, after many years of striving, a service book in the English tongue, designed to draw all men of goodwill into unity. The hope was not fulfilled.

In form the Act of Uniformity was like that previous Act of Uniformity known as the Act of the Six Articles. Refusal to adopt the new Book of Common Prayer, or agitation and speaking against it, involved the offender in penalties imposed by the State. Although a concurrent jurisdiction was explicitly allowed to the ecclesiastical courts, the justices of oyer and terminer and the chief officers of cities and boroughs were empowered to administer the Act. A parson was, for the second offence, to be imprisoned for a year and deprived *ipso facto* of all his spiritual promotions; for the third offence he might be imprisoned for life. But, whereas proceedings under the Act of the Six Articles were taken against innovators, proceedings under the Act of 1549 would be taken against those who resisted innovation and clung to books and practices which had an immemorial history. The reaction against the later Act was naturally more immediate and more profound, though less informed by deliberate and reasoned conviction, and less enduring than the opposition to the Act of Henry VIII. The rebellions of 1549 were not inspired by theological passion. The theological controversies were difficult and obscure, beyond the mental grasp of country clergy and peasants. The teaching of the new Prayer Book, in spite of its Protestant tendencies and colouring, was not clearly heterodox. Gardiner, who occupied himself at this time in elaborate writings upon the Sacrament, was prepared to accept the new book, and indeed was to jibe bitterly at the inconsistency between its implied theology and the archbishop's teaching on the Lord's Supper. Dryander explained to Bullinger that the 'absurdities' of the Book were due to the differences of opinion among the bishops. The real cause of the opposition of country clergy and Devonshire peasants was the proof which the Prayer Book seemed to give that all the agitations and change of the last few years really were going to end in a permanent cleavage between the past and the present, that the familiar was to give way to something strange, foreign, imposed. In their own way, surrounded by evidences of change, they felt as Peter Martyr did, that too much had been done for withdrawal to be possible, that things must move further. And, whereas Peter Martyr

and his friends rejoiced, they were stirred to anger and resentment. They had seen the monasteries go, they had
seen the royal commissioners breaking down images in
accordance with the injunctions of 1547 and the orders in
council of 1548; at this very time the chantries, witnesses
in nearly every church of the ever-present solicitude of the
living for the dead, of the religious bond in every gild and
fraternity, were being destroyed and their resources, the
gifts of local piety, confiscated to the crown. Their resistance was speedily suppressed; for while they were for
the time in earnest, others were hostile to them or luke-
warm or timid. But the persuasiveness of Cranmer and the
fiery rhetoric of the preachers failed to bring the country
to willing acquiescence in the new order. The persecu-
tions in Mary's reign, acting upon the mind of a new
generation, and gradual familiarity with new ways of life,
and with words which all could understand, and the opening up of new issues, in which the governing powers were
on the conservative side, and the rally of patriotic feeling
against external interference; all these were necessary before the Reformation settlement could be accepted as a
matter of course.

In the meanwhile, encouraged by the support of the
government, the Reformers went forward. The result was
the second Prayer Book, whose use was imposed in the
second Act of Uniformity in 1552. This Act illustrates
very clearly two tendencies which had been gathering
force during the previous three years. The first was a
growing concern with ecclesiastical order involving the
discipline of the laity. The second was the desire to interpret the meaning of the Sacrament of the Altar more
clearly in a Zwinglian sense. The Act, while retaining the
Act of 1549 in full force, was mainly concerned to secure
the diligent and faithful attendance of the people at their
parish churches at times of common prayer and other
services of the Church. It went farther in this direction
than any previous Act of Parliament.

The ecclesiastical authorities were exhorted to execute this part of the Act and were given 'full power and authority by this Act to reform, correct and punish' the recalcitrant 'by censures of the Church'. The civil authorities, whose duty it was to proceed against the clergy and laity under the earlier Act, still in force, were required in the second Act to deal with persons who were present at any other form of service than that authorized in the Prayer Book. Now here we have the development which had been anticipated with dismay by Gardiner, and we can see the triumph of the foreign ideas of discipline which were so distasteful to him, as to most Englishmen, and which he had attacked in his controversy with Bucer in Germany years earlier. It would doubtless be extravagant to suppose that Bucer's influence had been responsible for the change. Indeed, he thought that an intensive educational campaign by preachers was more important and would be more effective than a policy of legal discipline. Several active prelates, including Ridley, who had succeeded Bonner as bishop of London in 1550, Hooper, who, after much disputation about episcopal vestments, was consecrated bishop of Gloucester in March 1551, Coverdale, who was consecrated bishop of Exeter in August of the same year, were at work in their dioceses with firm convictions about the necessity of order. Ridley especially had for some time taken the lead in diocesan administration. But Bucer put the case for social and religious organization more clearly than anybody. Before he came to England Peter Martyr had bewailed to him the absence of men who were conversant with ecclesiastical order and government; and when he arrived and settled in Cambridge, he was much distressed by the state of the country. In his *De regno Christi*, presented to the King as a New Year's gift in 1551, he dealt in a very outspoken way with the need for reform. As I have said, we find little concern during this time with the nature of the Church and with the ideal relations of Church and State; but in Bucer's work we can see a lively concern for the formation of a well-ordered community worthy of the new truths now opened out to it. Like Latimer, he denounced the spoliation of the Church, the greed and indifference of the new nobility, the conversion by King and nobles alike of ecclesiastical wealth to secular uses or enjoyment. He was in favour of regulating social life—games, food, dress—of reforming the universities more drastically, and most of all, of a clear policy in regard to marriage and divorce. Concern with such matters was, of course, not new. Medieval secular legislation had dealt with, and the canon law was precise and minute about, most of them. But Bucer illustrates the policy, which most continental Reformers had in varying degree found to be necessary, of social and moral discipline in the light of the new religion; he felt the fervent desire to combine regulation with godly persuasion in an attempt to turn the self-contained State into a veritable Kingdom of God. His ideal was prophetic, and in due time was to develop into the conception of the State as subservient to the Church, the authorized guide in faith and morals. Gardiner had gone to the root of the matter when, in opposition to Bucer, he had deprecated minute interference in the moral and religious life of the individual, and had maintained that 'the contempt of human law was to be punished more heavily and more seriously than any transgression of the divine law'; or when he had rather cynically criticized Cranmer's enthusiasm for homilies and attendance at Church and the reading of the Scriptures by the laity. Whether he was right or wrong, he had a more accurate acquaintance than the Reformers had with the character of his countrymen. Nor were his countrymen the more disposed to welcome the new discipline because it was imposed upon them by a government led by the duke of Northumberland, one of the most cynical scoundrels who has ever held high office in England.

A letter from Bucer and Fagius, the Hebraist and

preacher, written to their friends in Strasbourg very soon
after their arrival in England in April 1549, shows that
within a few weeks of the passing of the first Act of Uniformity, Cranmer was looking forward to a revision of the
Prayer Book. The new-comers were entertained at Lambeth, with Peter Martyr, Dryander, Immanuel Tremellius
of Ferrara, and some 'godly Frenchmen'. The cause of religion and the state of the country were freely discussed.
The country needed teachers above all, for hitherto the
clergy had confined their duties chiefly to ceremonies.
Bucer considered that the definitions of rites and doctrines
were fairly satisfactory. He was assured that the concessions which had been made to antiquity and to human
infirmity, the eucharistic vestments, the use of candles and
chrism, were not superstitious and would only be retained
for a time. It was refreshing to find that all the services
were now read or sung in English, that the doctrine of
justification was purely and soundly taught and the
eucharist administered according to Christ's ordinance,
private masses having been abolished. Less moderate
critics, notably Hooper, were not so satisfied. Shortly before he was made bishop of Gloucester, Hooper, preaching
before the King, did not hesitate to demand the abolition
of useless and superstitious ceremonies and the revision of
the book, while Ridley, in the articles of his diocesan
visitation of May 1550, concentrated, not on the observance of the new order as a means of peace, but upon the
foolish practices which, though not illegal, too often accompanied it. He instructed his clergy, in the cause of a sensible uniformity, to provide a table in some convenient
place in the choir or sanctuary and to remove the altar. In
the course of the next month the grand altar in St. Paul's
and the altars in the London churches were destroyed. The
council, late in the year, adopted Ridley's view. The
bishops were commanded to replace altars by tables, on
the ground that the words altar and table were used in-
differently in the Prayer Book, which therefore gave no

superior sanction to the more superstitious use. Soon afterwards, in 1551, Ridley took a further step in repudiation of the sacrificial doctrine of the communion and, by officiating on various sides of the table or by placing it in different positions, made it clear that, in his view, there was no need for the table to be in a definite place. The actions and injunctions of the bishop of London were expressions of an impatient desire for change, which by the beginning of 1551 had affected king, council, and many others, as well as the foreign scholars in England. In January Sir John Cheke, the King's tutor, assured Peter Martyr that if the bishops did not move in the matter the King would make the necessary changes in the Prayer Book himself and impose his authority upon Parliament.[1] At last, at the end of 1551, a commission was appointed to revise the Prayer Book.[2]

The second Act of Uniformity was passed on 14 April 1552, but was not to come into force until 1 November. An episode which occurred during the interval showed how difficult united action was. In the previous year Hooper, after his appointment to Gloucester, had provoked a crisis at court by his refusal to wear the episcopal vestments at his consecration. After a tiresome controversy he was persuaded, or rather forced, to submit, but for a time the cause of uniformity was endangered by his obstinate conscience. He anticipated the famous Vestiarian controversy of Elizabeth's reign. In the summer of 1552 another crisis was created by the preacher John Knox, a protégé of the duke of Northumberland.

[1] *Memorials of Cranmer*, ii. 664, letter of Peter Martyr to Bucer, 10 Jan. 1551. Peter did not use the official style. He began the year on the 1 January.

[2] See the letter from the young Swiss student, John ab Ulmis, to Bullinger (Oxford, 10 Jan. 1552), in *Zürich Letters*, p. 444. Both Skinner, said by ab Ulmis to have been a member of the commission, and ab Ulmis refer to a convocation, but they do not appear to be using the word, in writing to their foreign correspondents, in the technical sense. Although Convocation met on 24 January 1552, it is impossible to say what share it had in the debates upon the second Prayer Book. It had no share in the work of revision.

Knox had already made a name in Scotland as a writer and, as one of the inmates of the castle of St. Andrews after the murder of Cardinal Beaton, he had been sent for a time to the French galleys which plied between the French and English coasts. Released in 1549, he served as a licensed preacher in Newcastle-on-Tyne, causing some trouble to the bishop of Durham, Tunstall, by his advanced teaching and practice. Like Hooper, he considered that it was idolatrous to receive the communion in a kneeling posture. If the Lord's Supper was a memorial service, to be held at a table placed in any position, the reception of the communion by participants on their knees was an inconsistent concession to the idolatrous doctrine of 'the sacrifice of the altar'. The form prescribed in the first Prayer Book made injunctions on the point unnecessary, but in the second Prayer Book the communicant was instructed to receive the bread and wine upon his knees. As Knox, and probably others, had encouraged the recipients of the Sacrament to sit, he regarded the rubric in the new Prayer Book as reactionary, and inconsistent with the tendency of the revision as a whole. Preaching at Windsor before the King in September 1552 he denounced the custom of kneeling. The King was disturbed by the thought that the new book contained any concession to the past which could be regarded as idolatrous. Cranmer, Ridley, and Peter Martyr were ordered to reconsider the matter. Again Cranmer succeeded in getting his way, and Knox, like Hooper, submitted, and urged his old congregation to submit, for the sake of 'uniform order to be kept and that for a time, in this Church of England'. But Cranmer's victory was not complete. When the Prayer Book was issued, it contained the famous Black Rubric, hastily inserted by the printer at the command of the Council, the rubric which, while it enjoins the kneeling posture for the sake of reverence and uniformity and as a signification of grateful acknowledgement, repudiates any suggestion of adoration, any concession to the belief that the bread and wine do not 'remain still in their very natural substance'. However modern theologians may interpret the words of the second Prayer Book, no doubt can be entertained of the intentions of the government of Edward VI.

IV. CRANMER, GARDINER, AND POLE

THE historical student of ecclesiastical change in England during Edward's reign cannot but wish that the King had lived and that Cranmer had been given a longer opportunity to pursue his policy. Would uniformity have been maintained, the differences between the Reformers been stilled, the incitement, which religious controversy always creates, to irreverence on the one hand and to conscientious resistance on the other, been overcome by measures of discipline and of the patient instruction which Bucer had urged? In 1552 the outlook was not a hopeful one. Feeling in the country was more excited and disturbed than it had been in 1547. Gardiner and Bonner were still in prison. Heath, bishop of Worcester, had been deprived of his see because he had refused to subscribe to the new Ordinal, or ordination services, which had been issued after the publication of the first Prayer Book. The hostility, which had broken out into rebellion, was still widespread. At the same time Cranmer, who had hoped for peace from the reception of Bucer's careful proposals for revision, the main source of the alterations in the second Prayer Book,[1] was beset by eager critics desiring to go further. The irreverence and scoffing at religious things which had disturbed the government in 1547 were revived by the endless discussions about the eucharist, to which noblemen listened as though they were at a play, by the destruction of images and altars, by the

[1] A good analysis of the relation between Bucer's *Censura*, or criticisms of the first Prayer Book, and the changes in the second Prayer Book, will be found in the papers on 'La transformation du culte anglican sous Édouard VI', contributed by the Abbé G. Constant to the *Revue d'histoire ecclésiastique* in 1911, xii, 251, 266. Bucer died before the second Prayer Book appeared. For the criticisms of continental reformers on the second book, cf. Smyth, op. cit., chapter vii. I have got much help from the works of these two writers.

CRANMER, GARDINER, AND POLE

wrangling about tables, by direct inducements to the profanation of the churches. Above all, the movement had fallen more and more into the hands of the Council and a few advisers, and was guided by coteries in private houses. Convocation was hardly considered; Parliament registered the decisions of the government. It is significant that the Act of January 1550, authorizing a new Ordinal, although it provoked some discussion in the House of Lords, approved beforehand a work which Parliament had not got before it. The Ordinal was to be devised by six prelates and six others learned in English law, appointed by the King; and it was to be 'set forth under the great seal of England before the 1st day of April next coming'. The forty-two Articles of Religion, the last important document compiled in this reign in order to secure uniformity on a clear basis of doctrinal statement, were prepared by a commission, submitted by council to the royal chaplains, revised by Cranmer again, and finally printed at the command of council with the false assertion that they had been agreed upon by the bishops and other learned men 'in the synod' (i.e. Convocation) at London.[1] When Cranmer protested he was told that the book was so entitled because it was set forth 'in the time of Convocation', although Convocation was not actually sitting in the summer of 1553. Finally, during these months Northumberland was busying himself with extensive plans for the further confiscation of ecclesiastical property, including the suppression of the great bishopric of Durham. When the King died, the government was not only acting in the unconstitutional way which Gardiner had foreseen early in the reign to be a danger; it was also, with the support of a few fanatics, pursuing a policy entirely opposed to the mind of the archbishop, and to the ideals of national reconstruction dear to men like Latimer and Bucer.

Yet, although the future must have seemed dark to the moderate reformers who had worked for a comprehensive

[1] This statement is found also in the Frankfurt edition of the Articles.

church, the religious expression of a united people, and although it looked very black to reformers of all shades of opinion when the policy of Queen Mary was revealed, they may well have felt that time was on their side. After the strange and moving incidents of the last twenty years England could never again be as it was when Wolsey died. The settlement of religion had become an affair of State, and no reaction was possible which had not parliamentary sanction. Many things had been done which could not be undone without violence to the interests, habits, and memories of the men who alone could undo them. New ways of looking at the great problems of social and ecclesiastical life had become familiar to reflective and nimble minds in council and parliament, in towns and universities, among clergy and laity alike. There were men to whom the practices of the early Church, however they regarded them, had become more familiar than the beliefs and usages of their fathers; others for whom German and Swiss innovations had no terrors; others still who were beginning to say that the past had no binding influence upon the present. Some men had been attracted by the possibilities of political and social reconstruction, and had no mind to let religious disputes stand in the way; others were beginning to realize keenly the difficulty of adjusting an orderly ecclesiastical system to the claims of a self-sufficing State. And for years past all had lived in an atmosphere of discussion about doctrine, rites, and ceremonies, a discussion which they knew was stirring the minds of men and women in half the countries of Europe. The movement of opinion could not have been maintained with so much intensity if it had not been inspired and spread by thinkers of ardent conviction, or strengthened by deep currents of genuine piety. Hard fighting and strong religious feeling went together, and we should do grave injustice to the generation which had succeeded the age of Sir Thomas More if we saw nothing in it but the excitement and the lust for theological battle. Combatants of all parties, however gentle and conciliatory they might be, knew that this was not a time for 'the delicate unrealities of the fashionable preacher'. The times were too dangerous and too momentous. The Reformers were in a minority, and might for a time be scattered or held down, but the sharper the effort to repress them, the more certain they could be of winning sympathy. The people as a whole had accepted with indifference the breach with Rome, the dissolution of the monasteries, the supremacy of the King, the authority in religious affairs of the secular power. They had resented the visitations, the destruction of chantries and altars, the attempts at an inquisitorial discipline, for these measures had affected their private life. They took little interest in, for they had no knowledge of, theological controversy, but they would be quick to resent the destruction of their neighbours by the agents of what they had come to regard as an alien power.

As we have seen, the developments of Edward VI's reign had revealed the inconsistencies and weaknesses of the view which was generally held by men in authority, whether conservative or reformist, about the relations between Church and State. Each of the two chief protagonists in the ecclesiastical politics of the years 1539 to 1552 was forced back to the fundamental question of conscience. What were they to do if their belief in the claim of the civil power to obedience came into conflict with their deepest convictions? The perplexities of Gardiner and the tragedy of Cranmer raised issues which are insoluble, just as the medieval dilemma from which they had escaped is insoluble. The claim of conscience in the end took the place of the claim of Rome. The issue presents little difficulty to the man who at heart is prepared to regard one authority as higher than the other, to obey his superior whatever happens, or to suffer any penalty for conscience' sake. But both Gardiner and Cranmer were men capable of strong private conviction, who had at the same time gladly and whole-heartedly accepted the royal supremacy. Their enemies, then and later, were satisfied to say that they were hypocrites, the one brutal, the other cowardly; but these are very short-sighted judgements. The two men were as unlike as two big men can be, but both were strong men with a sense of responsibility. And both were forced to choose between their allegiance to the State and their convictions about the Sacrament of the Lord's Supper. Gardiner's position was probably the more difficult, and it is unfortunate that in judging his earlier actions we have to rely mainly upon his apologia in the reign of Mary. He claimed then that he had tried to bring King Henry back to an understanding with the Papacy, and he naturally made the most of his opposition to the policy of Protector Somerset and Cranmer. His career, if studied in the light of what we can learn of his character and gather from his correspondence, was inconsistent, but it does not suggest that he was insincere. He was primarily a lawyer, learned in the canon law, an administrator, and a prelate. He was ambitious and self-confident, disliked anything that was factious or irregular, and despised the irresponsible people who were always ready with new ideas and new plans, but did not see where they were going. In the first days of the break with Rome, his best action was his defence of Convocation, his worst the bitter defence of the execution of bishop Fisher; yet, just as in maintaining the rights of Convocation he was asserting the com- patibility of two systems of law under one head, so in attacking the obstinacy of Fisher he was showing im- patience with a man who could not or would not dis- tinguish between the royal supremacy and the rest of the Catholic system. His theology was quite fixed, the organization of the Church was capable of adjustment to new conditions, the royal supremacy cut the knot in a legal tangle; and it was the duty of good ecclesiastics to fall into line. So far as he was concerned, in a world so full of dangerous and nonsensical tendencies, he would maintain the public order and put all his confidence in a

King whom he delighted to serve. Moreover, in his shrewd dealings with men, he had soon learned that a stiff-necked assertion of ecclesiastical rights would inevitably divide the spiritualty from the great laymen. He never forgot his conversations with Audley and other noblemen, and he came to insist, with all the zest of his legal mind, upon the importance of doing everything by rightful authority (*justa auctoritate*). If the clerical order could not maintain an independent position, then the Church and faith must be saved, and unity preserved, by the joint efforts of all right-thinking and sensible men in the highest court of the realm, or, in other words, by the King in Parliament. He was horrified by the lax, irresponsible attitude towards public order which he found in Germany, where for the sake of saving souls men would run the risk of social chaos. 'Many Commonwealths', he wrote, 'have continued without the Bishop of Rome's jurisdiction; but without true religion, and with such opinions as Germany maintained, no estate hath continued.' Hence his objection to the acts of Somerset and Cranmer after King Henry's death was aroused by his strong feeling that the government was lightly disregarding the implications, political and religious, of the recent settlement. He had been King Henry's chief and most intimate counsellor, and he could not keep silent. He would acquiesce, even obey as far as possible, but he would neither approve of measures which had not been carefully thought out under the direction of a King of mature years, nor would he surrender his conviction of the real presence in the eucharist, true by every criterion known to him, and the bulwark against the flood of dangerous, anti-social opinion. It is not hard to understand why, rather than see continue the state of things created by the second Act of Uniformity, he welcomed the reunion with Rome. Yet at no time did he utter a word in support of rebellion. On this point he was at one with Latimer and Cranmer. Just after his first imprisonment in the Fleet, he preached in the Cathedral of Winchester on

Palm Sunday 1548, 'that the life of a Christian man con-
sisteth chiefly in suffering of another man's will, and not his
own; and declared the duty of the subject to the rulers,
which was (as he said) to obey their rule and suffer their
power'. Resistance even to an infidel prince would be
wrong. Gardiner's view, so startling to the naturally Protestant mind, that disobedience to human authority deserved or should receive greater punishment than transgression of the divine law, sprang from the same passion for
public order and obedience. He meant that human law
itself was part of the divine law, and that sins and offences
with which human law did not concern itself were better
left to the judgement of God. They might or might not be
worse in God's sight than acts of disobedience to authority,
but that was not the point. The sole object of human law
is the maintenance of peace, quiet, and obedience. If an
'indifferent' or unimportant thing is forbidden, it is forbidden in the interest of peace and quiet and for no other
reason. Similarly, matters, however important, which do
not 'tend to the tearing asunder of the body of the Church
and to the overthrow of human society' are not appropriately included in human law.

Slothful, sluggish and idle fellows, he wrote, spoil themselves
by their laziness; they infringe God's law, yet they do not
touch the Commonwealth, nor do they disturb it, still less do
they cast it in confusion. But it is you who tread under foot all
order, you who trample down the common weal, while you
strive by covert ways to impair the authority of princes, and of
their edicts, even if in your turn you are willing to listen to the
truth. You adorn the authority of princes with insignificant
words, yet only so long as they accommodate their laws to your
own decisions, and follow your judgement in religious matters.
You have not abolished the authority of Rome throughout the
world, but you have appropriated it to yourselves and transferred it to Wittenberg. Let God himself teach us his truth, but
God's apt soldiers will not be those, who do not willingly submit to princes. And those men will never willingly submit who

discuss so anxiously of the manner of making laws and consider it of such moment that laws should be made for all men on things indifferent. Every man would gladly cast out, if he could, what he hates.[1]

The tract against Bucer, in which Gardiner's views are expounded, implies a conception of the Church as an institution held together by law, bound up with the political system, and strong enough to comprise all sorts and conditions of men.

It would be wrong to draw large generalizations from a single controversial pamphlet. The significance of Gardiner's observations lies in their casual revelation of the instinctive outlook of an important ecclesiastic. Gardiner had been trained in Wolsey's household. His practical attitude to the Church was characteristic of an active prelate of the fifteenth and sixteenth centuries. Whatever his theorizing may have been, he regarded the ecclesiastical system as part of the country's inheritance, a familiar aspect of English life. Such an attitude is neither medieval nor modern, but English, and has expressed the traditions of the Church of England until the present day. It helped to guide the English Reformation and in turn it gained in strength and definiteness from the new settlement, so that it lived through all the later movements, which have reacted against it. It helped to enervate the policy of Mary and Cardinal Pole, and it was resolutely set against the Genevan conception of the Church-State and the separatist conception of the Church as a self-disciplined independent expression of Christian experience. The Church comprehended all, yet depended on none; was everywhere, but inseparable from the common life. The difference between Gardiner and his successors is that while he wished to retain, as part of the order of things, the traditional forms

---

[1] Pierre Janelle, *Obedience in Church and State; three political tracts by Stephen Gardiner* (1930), p. 209. In one place I have ventured to alter Mr. Janelle's translation.

and beliefs, and saw in them the guarantee of truth and order, they have taken their stand upon the Thirty-nine Articles as fundamental.

Cranmer's attitude to civil power was simpler and more logical than Gardiner's. More persuasive and less forceful than his rival, he was more independent in mental outlook, and did not feel the need of his stubborn reservations. He rejoiced in the royal supremacy, partly because he regarded it as natural and scriptural, partly because under its guidance the religious life of England might be organized in what he regarded as a truly scriptural way. His mind was bold, yet he was moderate and cautious in temperament. In matters of doubt or indifference he preferred to cling to the old, yet he was curious and anxious to consider the new. His moral fibre was not so strong as his mental honesty, and he acquiesced in many things which he cannot have approved. Perhaps the clearest impression of him is given by his views on ecclesiastical authority. He was deeply concerned about the organization of the Church and with uniformity. Most of the important documents compiled between 1539 and 1553 were drafted by him or under his guidance; the revisions of the canon law, liturgies, catechisms, homilies, forms of worship, articles of religion. His *Ordinal*, if we consider the circumstances, is a very masterly work of conservative statesmanship, so careful in its phrasing that only the expert theologian could detect its difference from the old. 'There is no difference between it and ours', wrote the Venetian ambassador, 'except that the ordinands renounce the authority of the pope.' It would seem that he was more concerned than Gardiner was that the Church should have its own system, and be an *imperium in imperio*. In fact, he was more free to adopt this policy just because he did not feel Gardiner's reservations. As early as 1540 he gave very frank expression to his views on the appointment and power of bishops and priests. A list of searching questions had been submitted to a number of bishops and divines. They comprised the following: 'whether the apostles, lacking a higher power, as in not having a Christian King among them, made bishops by that necessity or by authority given them by God?'; 'whether a bishop hath authority to make a priest by the Scripture or no? and whether any other, but only a bishop, may make a priest?'; 'whether a bishop or a priest may excommunicate, and for what crimes? and whether they only may excommunicate by God's law?' The replies given to these questions varied greatly, as one would expect. They raised the issue which in modern times, since the days of the Oxford Movement, is the most momentous issue in the Church of England, of the continuity of the Church, whether or not, as an organized and visible body, its nature and authority depend upon a continuous ministry of bishops and priests whose power has been transmitted to them, independently of any other authority, by Christ Himself. They are fundamental questions, and they might be answered in ways which were hardly consistent with the statutory authority of King Henry. Some of the replies given, though cautious in their wording, maintained that grace was derived from Christ and the Apostles. On the position of the prince they were silent or tended to equivocate. This view, combined with an assertion of the strict limitation of episcopal and priestly authority to the exercise of a 'moderate' power, subject to the ends for which God ordained it, was generally accepted in the sixteenth century, without assertion of any divine right residing in the Church and its ministers as an independent society.[1]

To revert to the questions of 1540. Bonner, the new bishop of London, thought that 'if Christian princes had been there, they should have named by right, although the Apostles made Bishops by the Law of God; that a bishop duly appointed had authority to make a bishop

[1] It was expounded by Queen Elizabeth in 1559 and is implied in the Thirty-nine Articles.

and priest, also that consecration was required (and yet the truth of this I leave to higher judgements)'; and that, as the Canon Law teaches, the power of excommunication belongs to the bishop and, in less degree, to priests. Cranmer was much bolder:

All Christian princes have committed unto them immediately of God the whole care of all their subjects, as well concerning the administration of God's word for the cure of souls, as concerning the ministration of things political and civil governance. And in both these ministrations they must have sundry ministers under them to supply that which is appointed to their several offices.

Hence the ministers of God's word, like civil ministers, are appointed by the laws and orders of kings and princes. . . . 'And there is no more promise of God that grace is given in the committing of the ecclesiastical office, than it is in the committing of the civil office.' Consecration is not required by Scripture. Christian princes have the power, as a bishop has, to make a priest, and in the absence of ecclesiastics (for example, after the conquest of an infidel country), could preach, and appoint priests. Moreover:

A bishop or a priest by the Scripture is neither commanded nor forbidden to excommunicate, but where the laws of any region giveth him authority to excommunicate, there they ought to use the same in such crimes as the laws have such authority in; and where the laws of the region forbiddeth them, there they have none authority at all; and they that be no priests may also excommunicate, if the law allow them thereunto.

In short, the organization of the Church under right authority was, in Cranmer's view, a matter of expediency. The teaching of Scripture did not deal with these things. Hence he might well approach them with an accommodating mind. At the same time he had no objection to non-scriptural rites and ceremonies as such; indeed, they

were essential to the maintenance of order and uniformity. In his answer to Knox and the unquiet spirits
'which can like nothing but that is after their own fancy',
and who would still find faults in the Prayer Book, although it were made every year anew, he denounced the
error that what is not commanded in Scripture is against
Scripture: 'This saying is a subversion of all order as well
in religion as in common policy.' In the same spirit he
approached the ideal, to which he periodically devoted his
mind between 1537 and 1552, of an understanding between the reformed churches of England and the Continent. In 1537 he still believed in the real presence in the
Sacrament, and he urged the Reformers to unite on this
solid rock. He deplored their tendency, in confuting
papistical errors, to tread down the wheat with the tares,
in other words, to 'do violence to the authority of the
ancient doctors and chief writers in the Church of Christ'.
And, later on in the same letter to the Swiss scholar,
Joachim Vadian, he wrote, 'we should easily convert even
the Turks to the obedience of our gospel, if only we would
agree among ourselves and unite together in some holy
confederacy'. After his conversion to the views of Ridley
and Bucer, he made several attempts to arrange conferences with a view to a common statement of the reformed theology in reply to the dangerous movement at
work in the Council of Trent. In a letter of March 1552,
to Calvin, he says: 'They are, as I am informed, making
decrees respecting the worship of the host; whereupon we
ought to leave no stone unturned, not only that we may
guard others against this idolatry, but also that we may
ourselves come to an agreement upon the doctrine of the
Sacrament.' Anticipating the objection that the agreement could not be effected without the aid of princes, he
assured Melanchthon that the King of England was
anxious to help.

Here we come very close to the moral dilemma which
lay in wait for Cranmer. Suppose the prince would not

help, or was even hostile to the Reformers' theology? In spite of his steadily advancing opinions, Cranmer had retained the goodwill of Henry VIII, and in 1552 he could rely upon the support of the quick-witted boy who had succeeded Henry. But in Mary's reign he was ordered, not to acquiesce, but to recant his conviction about the Lord's Supper. The fact that he was brought to trial before the Pope's commissioners and that his death was determined upon in any event no doubt made the final victory of conscience easier for him; but his adversaries had not spared him the dilemma. They urged the argument that in resisting he was resisting his prince; and for a time he was overwhelmed by the reflection that he owed the same obedience to Mary which he had given to Henry and Edward. He was, as one shrewd observer had once observed, 'plain, tractable, gentle, mild, loath to displease'. The dilemma was a real one. But as he had more than once faced Henry in the past, so in the end he faced himself, and, after one humiliating lapse, he stood fast.

It was not his death, but his victory over himself, which mattered. He made it clear that, however close the relations between Church and State might be, religion in England was not and could never be entirely subdued to public policy. For Cranmer was much more than an archbishop prepared to die for his faith; he was the most thorough-going advocate of the supremacy of the prince, under whose rule, expressed in customary ways, civil and ecclesiastical ministers supervised, each in his own place, and each with the same kind of authority, the functions of society. He did not believe that he as bishop had any peculiar grace. But he had from his youth believed in the Scriptures as the guide to truth and the natural law; and, as he had repudiated the claim of the Catholic Church to interpret it, he could do no other at the last but depend upon himself.

The study of character in the days of Henry VIII and Edward VI is more fascinating than in almost any period of English history. The times were so disturbed, and life was so dangerous. Men in high places could not feel safe, like the poet Wyatt, who, free from the perils and intrigues of court, rejoiced that he was in 'Kent and Christianity'. Everything changed when King Henry, bringing with him a sense of dreadful and capricious power, came into the room with his little darting glance. Nobody could be certain of the morrow in the days of Somerset and Northumberland. Cranmer, a man of quiet, observant ways, had to live with a cautious intensity not often required of statesmen. As Carlyle says of John Sterling, 'it was not as a ghastly phantom, choked in controversies, scepticisms, agonised self-dealings, that this man appeared in life'. A close, very human relation with the world about them links him with Gardiner, with his love of business, and his magnificence and 'merry tales', and Ridley and Latimer and Heath and Thirlby and all the other actors in the uneasy movements of these years. And, far away in Italy or passing on fruitless missions from one country to another, another man, as able as any of these and nobler than all, was waiting his time to enter on the scene. Reginald Pole was nine years old when Henry VIII began his reign. His mother, the Countess of Salisbury, was related to the royal house, and from his early years Pole enjoyed the favour and support of the King. He was of gentle disposition, sparing of speech, meditative, but strong-willed and single-minded, of frugal habits and austere with himself. He studied in Oxford, Paris, and Padua, where he kept house as a great nobleman. He had been taught by Linacre, and was on familiar terms with the chief Italian scholars. Erasmus saluted him as an ornament of scholarship (*studiorum decus*).[1] From the first

[1] Allen, *Erasmi Epistolae*, No. 1675 (vi. 283). Erasmus had brought together Pole and the Polish nobleman, John a Lasco, who was afterwards superintendent of the Strangers' Church in London, and as the friend of Cranmer, Peter Martyr, Bucer, and others, had considerable influence upon ecclesiastical movements in the reign of Edward VI. See Smyth, op. cit., chapter vi.

his mother had taught him to prepare for an ecclesiastical
career, and after Wolsey's death he might have been the
archbishop of York, but he did not take deacon's orders
until he was made a cardinal by Pope Paul III at the end
of 1536, and he first celebrated Mass as a priest on the day
of Cranmer's execution in March 1556, less than three
years before his death. Yet while he lived so long as a layman, he had very soon made the religious well-being of
England the main passion of his life. Like Sir Thomas
More, he had dwelt much with the English Carthusians
and not a little of their spirit breathed through his later
life. He firmly resisted the incessant attempts of King
Henry to win him to his side. Henry, indeed, had a
genuine affection and unusual respect for him, and
anxiously awaited his judgement. His wrath at Pole's
ultimate defection, shown by his acceptance of the car-
dinalate shortly after the completion of his treatise on the
unity of the Church,[1] smouldered all the more fiercely,
and found vent in the most savage and merciless of his
violent deeds, the attainder and execution of the cardinal's mother and eldest brother in 1541. Pole by this
time was one of the leading men in the Papal court, the
close friend of Contarini, and, like him, one of the little
group anxious to reform the Church from within. In spite
of his absorption in English affairs, he was anything but
an ecclesiastical schemer. His mind was open to all the
best influences at work within the Church. If he repudiated the Lutheran doctrine of justification by faith he
had none the less, with Contarini, experienced the blind-
ing revelation of justifying grace. He had convinced himself, by ardent study, of the claims of a single united
church under Papal guidance. As events were to show, he
had lost touch with England and was not really fitted to
grapple with the strange situation of English affairs after
King Edward's death. He had become too set in his ways,
and, though never a bigot, was too single-minded in pur-

[1] Written for King Henry's private use, and not published till 1554.

pose. Yet in earlier life he had speculated much about the social order, and in his freedom from prejudice was not unlike Sir Thomas More. If the statements of his former companion and secretary, Thomas Starkey, as faithfully reflect his ideas as they profess to do, his views were nearer to those of Latimer than to those of Gardiner. In his mind the medieval ideal of the prince was enriched by the vision of a government, whose opportunities of tyranny were rigidly removed, engaged upon a programme of social reconstruction. Clergy as well as laity must be subdued to the object of creating a healthy, rich, industrious, and intelligent community.[1]

Such was the man who, after long and vexatious delays, arrived in England as Papal legate in November 1554 and pronounced the absolution of the erring country on St. Andrew's Day (30 November). The reconciliation of England with the Church seemed to be complete, yet in fact the cardinal could do little. The contrast between the ideals of this great man, who at one time had just missed the Papacy, and the compromises to which he had to submit and political difficulties in which he was involved, gives us the measure of the changes which Henry VIII's policy had worked in England. Pole was faced by even greater obstacles than the will of Parliament. He was suspected in imperial and Spanish quarters on the one hand, and exposed on the other to criticism and backbiting in the Roman court. During Mary's reign conflict of interests between her husband Philip of Spain and the Papacy became so great that the two powers were involved in open warfare over Italian affairs. In consequence Pole's position as legate of the Holy See in part of Philip's dominions was threatened, and, in spite of the representations of Mary's ambassador, his commission was revoked (1557). As Cranmer's successor in the primacy, he could still continue to direct ecclesiastical affairs in England, but forces

[1] Starkey, *The Dialogue between Cardinal Pole and Thomas Lupset*, written 1536–8, first published for the Early English Text Society in 1878.

in Rome were working against him. When he died, on the same day as Mary (17 Nov. 1558), he was under sentence of recall to Rome and had for some months been engaged in protesting against the action of Pope Paul IV and defending himself against the charge of heresy, from which he had suffered in the past and to which men of keen reforming minds and uncompromising piety have always been exposed.

Political rivalry in Europe had allowed Henry VIII and the advisers of his successor a free hand. The political calculations of the Emperor and his son Philip of Spain led them to work for as easy a reconciliation as possible between England and Rome. Before he was allowed to land in England Pole had been compelled to acquiesce in a compromise which was already effective. He had himself urged upon Mary the importance of a frank and personal understanding with her Parliament, but he does not seem to have realized how far the Lords and Commons would go in their insistence upon the present state of things. The more practical people in Rome were wiser than he when they declared that the confiscation of ecclesiastical property was not too great a price to pay for the reconciliation of a heretical country. No church lands were restored save the few surrendered at the bidding of conscience, and nearly all these were surrendered by the Queen. Parliament insisted upon incorporating in a statute the Papal bull which dispensed the holders of Church property from the duty to give them up. The Pope never got back his annates or first-fruits, although the Queen refused them. The reunion with Rome was achieved by the repeal of anti-papal legislation and on the petition of both houses of Parliament. Throughout her reign Mary was unable to control her parliaments, and had much difficulty in composing a council in which she could confide. On the other hand, the independent authority of Convocation was restored, and between November 1555 and February 1556 Pole held a legatine synod, comprising the convocations of both provinces, in which the plan of a *reformatio Angliae* was drawn up. Above all, jurisdiction over heresy was fully restored to the ordinaries and the ecclesiastical courts. Early in her reign (March 1554) Mary had commanded the bishops to proceed diligently and earnestly in the repression of heresy and the restoration of order in the Church. Articles were circulated for their guidance, including one which forbade them to use in any document the phrase implying royal supremacy (*regia autoritate fulcitus*). They were to proceed 'without fear of any presumption to be noted on your part, or danger to be incurred of any such our laws as of your doings . . . might anywise grieve you'. The penalties of praemunire could be invoked in Mary's reign against those who took to a church court a suit regarding the confiscated property of the Church, but in its proceedings against heresy the Church was free and could rely upon the support of the civil power.[1] The result was a cleavage between laity and clergy; the ashes of three hundred martyrs lay between them. The episcopal bench and the ranks of the clergy could be purged, but the laity remained as they had always been. When Elizabeth came to the throne Convocation was more united in its support of Rome than it had been even in 1530, but whatever sense of relief the reunion with Rome had brought to a distracted people had entirely disappeared.

Neither Pole nor Gardiner, who died in November 1555, had taken much share in the extirpation of heresy. Both were fortunate in the time of their death. But Pole, unlike Gardiner, was committed heart and soul to the traditional independence of the Church. He brought to its defence the objective conviction and missionary fervour

---

[1] In February 1557 Philip and Mary issued a commission to a number of bishops, laity, and learned men to investigate, through juries and witnesses, various ecclesiastical matters, including heresy. Suspected heretics were to be handed over to the ordinaries. The form of the commission, however, is very interesting and connects the practice of Elizabeth's with that of earlier reigns.

which the shock of the Reformation had produced in earnest and godly men, especially men who had themselves felt the force of the new teaching, and were themselves reformers. In the painful correspondence which passed between Cranmer, in the time of his trial, and the Cardinal, who replied on behalf of the Queen, this issue of the independence of the Church has a large place. The clergy, Cranmer wrote,

seek to maintain the pope, whom they desired to have their chief head, to the intent that they might have, as it were, a kingdom and laws within themselves, distinct from the laws of the crown, and wherewith the crown may not meddle, and so being exempted from the laws of the crown, might live in this realm like lords and kings without damage or fear of any man so that they please their high and supreme head at Rome.

In his reply Pole unhesitatingly affirmed the high view which Papalist writers had expounded in the thirteenth and fourteenth centuries. Since the days of Grosseteste no Englishman had spoken with such vigour in this strain. He argued that the law of heresy derived from the Canon Law and that even in recent times no one had been condemned for the crime of heresy 'by the mere justice that cometh from the temporal laws'. He dealt with Cranmer's protest against foreign jurisdiction and pointed out that historically no 'spiritual man' had been put to execution until he had been surrendered to the secular arm according to canon law. He then explained how foolish, how inconsistent it was with the providence of God and the very fabric of society to describe the papacy as a *foreign* power:

The Pope's power can no more be called foreign power, coming not of man alone but of Him that is God and Man . . . than may be called a foreign power, that the soul of man coming from heaven hath in the body generate in earth. And so be it in the politic body of this realm, ruled with politic laws, founded by man's reason that be called temporal laws, which cometh from princes and governors temporal, to them coming the Pope's laws spiritual, doth no other, but that the soul in the body, to give life to the same, to confirm and strengthen the same.

If ever, in our impatience with the abstract and unreal, we are disposed to dismiss the Papalist view of the re-lations between human and spiritual, common and canon law as empty and innocuous verbiage, it is worthy of remembrance that this view was expounded as an ex-pression of the deepest truth of the universe by one great Englishman to another at one of the greatest moments in English history. The legate, after years of exile, attainted as a traitor, had at last seen his dreams come true. In his eyes Cranmer was doomed for no mere breach of law, but because he had broken his oath to the Pope, repudiated the most sacred truths of the Catholic faith, and derided as an alien power the channel through which Christ, as soul within body, worked beneficently upon the society of mankind. For the first, and also the last, time the ideals of the Counter-Reformation, in their purest, most austere, and most ruthless form, were upheld in England by the highest authority in the Church. And they were expounded to a man in prison, who had done more than any other man to resist them.

The more prosaic view was that the temporary recon-ciliation with Rome was an unfortunate parliamentary experiment. In the defence of his *Apology for the Church of England* published in 1567 in answer to Thomas Harding, Bishop Jewel pointed out that it was beside the mark to scoff at 'parliament religion'. God's everlasting truth came from God, not from parliaments, although historically re-ligion in England had always been, in a sense, parliament religion. 'With like sobriety and gravity of speech ye might have said, Our fathers in old times had a parlia-ment Christ.' Parliaments, it is true, are uncertain and

E

may err, as in Queen Mary's reign, when the Pope was received by assent of Parliament. Moreover, he was received under conditions—'otherwise his holiness had gone home again'.[1] This is another view of English history.

[1] *Works of John Jewel*, edited by R. W. Jelf (Oxford, 1848), vi. 215–17.

V. THE ELIZABETHAN CHURCH

REGARDED in the light of later history, the 'Elizabethan Settlement' deserves and has received as
much attention as any other movement in this
all-important period. It can be studied minutely from year
to year in State papers, correspondence, pamphlets, controversial treatises, and literature. From the point of view
of this essay, it must be regarded as an epilogue to the
dramatic and poignant conflicts of the previous reigns.
When Mary died all the issues had been raised or could
easily be foreseen. The main fabric of the Church in
England stood unshaken, the instruments of its government were at hand. Its title deeds, statutes, and ordinances
were all prepared. It was the task of Queen Elizabeth and
her advisers to dispel the alarms and uncertainties about
its future, to open its doors as widely as possible, and to
deal firmly with its adversaries. Other ways than theirs
might be ideally better and stir the passionate enthusiasm
of earnest men; but the lines of advance were already too
firmly drawn to be abandoned. Hence, under the control
of Queen, Privy Council, and Ecclesiastical Commissioners, the Church gradually stood clear, freed from the
dust and noise and scaffolding raised by the restorers and
renovators. To onlookers it was a great ancient monument,
not merely protected by the State, but the home of such
far-reaching and vital activities as to require the control
of the State. It was a department of State invested with
prestige or ineffectiveness or shameful slavery as different
minds might regard it; and time has made the investiture
venerable.

In Elizabeth's reign the Church had a medieval constitution, and a comprehensive liturgy, in which ancient,
medieval, Lutheran, and Zwinglian elements were welded
together in beautiful English. The theology most prevalent

among its ministers was Calvinist. Any independence which it might gradually acquire in men's minds had to find expression in the course of controversy, as its apologists laboured the apostolic and patristic authority for the episcopal system against Presbyterians within the Church and Separatists who repudiated it, or as they maintained the historical validity of its orders and its relations with the State against its Papal critics.

The successive changes of opinion were noted with delicate accuracy by Bacon about 1589. First the party which maintained the existing government of the Church laid stress upon the indifferent character of the ceremonies disliked by the Puritans; there might be imperfections, but these were not 'with strife to be pulled up lest it might spoil and supplant the good corn'. In the next stage they stiffly argued against change as unnecessary and dangerous to the unity of the existing order: 'Thence (exasperate through contentions) they are fallen into a direct condemnation of the contrary part as of a sect'. From this position it was an easy step to question the standing of the non-episcopal churches on the Continent and the validity of their orders. About the year 1588 the government was being pressed to take account of the tendency of thought among the bishops, and was especially urged to make them declare their minds on the origin of episcopal authority; was it God's own ordinance, or 'the direct grant from her Majesty by virtue of her supreme government'? Opinions were sought from learned civilians as well as from the bishops. The danger was not, in fact, very great. Bancroft, bishop of London, who had lately preached a disturbing sermon which caused much consternation, did not venture to deny the validity of the orders of continental Protestants, and Whitgift, the archbishop, fell into line with current opinion, namely that whatever divinity resided in the episcopal system was not, so to speak, innate, but attached to the maintenance of order or degrees of authority, for such an end accorded with the mind of Christ. Episcopacy was not necessary, therefore, and the episcopal dignity and authority owed much, if not all, to the privileges and powers granted by secular rulers.[1] It is true, that in the course of time apologetic analysis evolved a conviction that the Church, as an expression in society of the commands of Christ and the working of the Holy Spirit, had a self-sufficing unity of its own, was in fact that state within a state which Cranmer had disowned in the last days of his life. But there is very little trace of this conviction in Elizabeth's reign, nor has it ever found general support even among those who maintain the superior authority of episcopal government and would shrink in horror from the suggestion that their strength did not come direct from God.[2] Indifference to it was the gravamen laid against the Church by the Tractarians a hundred years ago.

On the other hand, a different tendency making for independence can be traced in Elizabeth's reign. This had its origin in the nature of the relations between Church and State. Was not the prince the head of the Church by divine right? Did he not owe his authority in the Church to grace just as the Church's ministers did when they ordained priests or dispensed the Sacraments? Should he not be regarded as part of the Church, just as in other capacities he was part of the State? The Supremacy Act of 1534 had confirmed, not granted, the right of Henry

---

[1] See appendix vi in Child's *Church and State under the Tudors*, pp. 293–304. It is curious that Whitgift's statements, given by Strype, are verbally identical in one place with the opinion written for Burghley by Dr. John Hammond, a civil lawyer and one of the high commissioners. Perhaps Hammond's statement had been submitted to Whitgift as a model, for it was written in Nov. 1588, six months before Sir Francis Knollys urged Burghley to insist on episcopal declarations about the new views (*Burghley Papers*, iii. 366–70, 412–13). By far the clearest exposition of the definitely Protestant view was made by Andrew Willet in his great work, *Synopsis Papismi*, first issued in 1593. See especially, in the edition of 1634, pp. 277 and following. On Bancroft's famous sermon of Feb. 1589, cf. R. Usher in *Mélanges Bémont* (Paris, 1913), pp. 539–47. It was misrepresented by contemporaries.

[2] The chief exception is the treatise on the *Perpetual Government of Christ's Church* (1593), by Thomas Bilson, afterwards bishop of Winchester.

VIII to be the supreme head of the Church of England.
It had asserted that 'the King's Majesty is and ought to be
the supreme head'. Hence Queen Mary had not power to
repudiate the title, and Queen Elizabeth did not require
an Act to restore it. This view seems to have been taken by
Parliament itself in the turmoil of opinion after Elizabeth's
accession,[1] and indeed the Supremacy Act of 1559 did not
formally invest her with the title. It re-enacted the legislation, repealed in Mary's reign, against all foreign jurisdiction, and comprised a form of oath in which, in accordance with the Queen's wishes, she was described as the
'only supreme governor in this realm . . . as well in all
spiritual and ecclesiastical things or causes as temporal'.
Moreover, in this reign the commissioners empowered
under the letters patent of the Queen to deal with ecclesiastical matters gradually assumed the character of a
permanent body which developed a judicial procedure of
its own and was styled a court. In the eyes of common
lawyers the Court of High Commission became suspect as
a creation of the Crown, dealing with cases which might
appropriately be dealt with by the courts of common law.
The tendency to go behind the parliamentary sanction
given to the position of the Crown was natural and in its
way logical; it coincided with a political tendency to exalt
the Crown, for whereas in earlier days Parliament had
been the means of expression of the royal will, a customary
assertion of the harmony between King and people, it
now began to take a line of its own on ecclesiastical and
political affairs. Men concerned in administration, or
given to the wide study of politics and history, urged, in
reply, that in the long run lawyers and parliaments were
means, not ends. 'God forbid,' said Bacon, 'upon pretence
of liberties or laws, government should have any head not
the King.' Moreover, the Church was vitally concerned
in maintaining the prerogatives of the Crown, for it was

[1] See the interesting narrative in Pollard, *Political History of England, 1549–
1603*, pp. 201 ff.

vitally concerned to rebut the arguments of Rome. The doctrine of the divine right of Kings, as the late Dr. Figgis pointed out, sprang directly and intimately from the controversy with Rome. An English bishop could not find a substitute for the Pope in a Puritanical House of Commons or seek protection in the arguments of Erastian lawyers. In Henry VIII's days this sort of doctrine had been dangerous, for then the lay supporters of the King feared the bishops: they had no intention of letting them evade that sword of Damocles, *praemunire*. The times were soon to come when the argument would be more dangerous still, and an archbishop would precede his King on the scaffold. But in Elizabeth's reign, when the Crown was threatened from without and patriotic feeling ran higher and the Queen was the object of an almost superstitious loyalty, the danger was not great. Many Englishmen, indeed, in their dislike at once of episcopal activity and Puritan interference, turned to the Crown as the natural safeguard of the normal man against ecclesiastical fussiness or ambition. The numerous Tudor families whose greatness was due to their connexion with the Crown, and was built on wealth acquired in the Court of Augmentations, felt no doubt whatever on this point. The second Lord North, the head of one of these families, wrote to the bishop of Ely in 1575:

Suffer me, my Lord, I pray you, to put you in mind who it is that you deny;[1] it is our dread sovereign lady, our most gracious and bountiful Mistress, who hath abled you even from the meanest estate that may be unto the best bishopric in England. . . . She is our God on earth; if there be perfection in flesh and blood, undoubtedly it is in her Majesty. For she is slow to revenge and ready to forgive. And yet, my lord, she is right King Henry, her father. . . .

[1] Cox, Bishop of Ely, had refused to grant a lease to the Queen. North's letter is in the *Burghley Papers*, ii. 121 (*Historical MSS. Commission*). Cox is said elsewhere to have had very exalted ideas of the part which bishops should play in the State.

Although we can trace in Elizabeth's reign the various strands which were combined later in the argument for divine right, it would be a mistake to conclude that there was much difference in fact between the Elizabethan and the earlier settlement of the Church. Like the change of title from Supreme Head to Supreme Governor, the tendencies which I have noted had a prophetic, not an immediate significance. They were latent in any settlement attempted by the State, but even to this day they have never found unimpeded expression. The Elizabethan settlement was as much the work of the Crown in Parliament as the Henrician or the Edwardian. The difference lay in the clearer allocation of functions, and in the steadier influence of the Crown. Convocation, for example, though its Catholic protests were disregarded in 1559, adopted, with slight changes, the Forty-two articles of Cranmer, and issued them in 1563 as the Thirty-nine articles. On several occasions during the reign Convocation agreed upon canons which defined and regulated practice and discipline in all kinds of ecclesiastical matters. In 1604, after Elizabeth's death, with King James's full encouragement and consent, it compiled a comprehensive series of canons, which was practically a series of definitions of the nature of the Church as true and apostolic, the denial of which was to involve excommunication. This was the culminating point in the efforts of Bancroft, bishop of London and afterwards archbishop of Canterbury, to secure complete order and unity in the Church. Yet, if we look at the other side of the matter, we find many obstacles in the way of Convocation, preventing it from becoming, subject to the royal consent, the independent legislative body of the Church. An act of 1571 was required to make subscription to the Articles compulsory upon 'priests or ministers', and this Act significantly imposed subscription only to the Articles which concern the true Christian Faith and the Doctrine of the Sacraments. Until 1597 the canons of Convocation did not receive the royal assent and were not enforced. The canons of 1604, which involved laymen in the penalties of excommunication, were attacked in Parliament, and, as affecting laymen, were not regarded as binding in the secular courts. Indeed, the revival of Convocation was in Elizabeth's reign largely due to the acquiescence of a Puritan Parliament, which desired to see a better state of discipline, not to any deliberate assertion of power. Under Elizabeth's cautious rule, the check came from the Crown, whereas in James's reign it came from the Puritan forces, parliamentary and legal, which resented the new episcopal pressure. In the same way Elizabeth and her advisers were quick to reprimand the bishops if they showed too eager a desire to enforce uniformity for the sake of doing so, without regard to circumstances. The placable Parker, who had helped to smooth over the difficulties created early in the reign by the fanatical opponents of vestments, was a more congenial archbishop, even if he had to be prodded occasionally, than the legal-minded Whitgift, who believed that laws should always be enforced. The times were very difficult; it was expedient, indeed necessary, to have statutes and injunctions and 'advertisements' in reserve, and on occasion to enforce them rigidly; but ecclesiastical discipline should always be subservient to political good sense, and of this the Queen and her ministers were the proper judges. When in 1584 Whitgift and eight other bishops issued Articles for the control of preachers, Burghley told him that 'according to my simple judgement, this kind of proceeding is too much savouring of the Romish inquisition, and is rather a device to seek for offenders than to reform any'. When again, in 1595, Whitgift assembled a gathering of bishops and clergy at Lambeth to deal with a little anti-Calvinist party at Cambridge, and compiled a number of Calvinistic propositions against free-will, the Queen told him, through Sir Robert Cecil, that 'she misliked that any allowance had been given by his Grace and the rest of any such points to be disputed; being a matter tender and dangerous to weak, ignorant minds'. She took exactly the same line with the Commons when they tried to press the settlement in a Presbyterian direction. The modern writers who think that the powers of Church and State, of Queen and Council and hierarchy, were combined in a fierce suppression of every kind of recusancy, have not surveyed the whole field. Elizabeth held Gardiner's view, that the task of government, in the administration of law, should not be complicated by fussy interference, that the people in a critical age should not be provoked by minute investigation into their conduct and opinions. She had to hold the balance even between bishops, Parliament, excited controversialists of all kinds. If disorder became too dangerous, the law must be enforced, but provocation was at all costs to be avoided. As she did not feel so strongly as Gardiner had felt about theological matters, she was able to act upon this view with more consistency, and, as her government was strong and national, with more success than had been possible in the middle of the century.

'God save us', said Archbishop Parker, 'from such a visitation as Knox has attempted in Scotland; the people to be orderers of things.' Popular or clerical control in the sixteenth century meant persecution, and Elizabeth could not afford, even if she had wished, to persecute. Hence she, like her father, must have the control of jurisdiction, and have it by parliamentary authority. The Act of Supremacy (1559) united and annexed to the imperial crown of the realm such jurisdictions 'as by any spiritual power or authority have heretofore been or may lawfully be exercised or used for the visitations of the ecclesiastical state and persons, and for reformation, order and correction of the same, and of all manner of errors, heresies, schisms, abuses, offences, contempts and enormities'. 'Heresy and schism' were henceforward, as in the litany, conjoined in the minds of Englishmen. If the danger of schism was far more practical and immediate than the danger of heresy, this was not only due to the return to England of the exiles who had sharpened their opinions in Switzerland and Frankfort, or to the controversies which disturbed the pupils and lecture rooms of Cambridge; it was due also to the careful definition of heresy in an Act of Parliament. In the confused debates of 1558–9, one point became clear, that the definition of heresy was not to be left to a victorious party, but was to be decided according to rules laid down by the highest authority in the State. England was saved from the heresy hunters because conformity, not opinion, was made the chief test of obedience. The Act of Supremacy provided that 'no manner of order, Act, or determination, for any matter of religion or cause ecclesiastical' made by the present Parliament should be judged to be heretical or schismatical. This was, no doubt, an attempt of Parliament to protect itself, but it reveals a curiously insular and secular attitude to the nature of heresy. In another clause the Act forbade any commissioners of the Crown, appointed to administer the Act, to judge 'any matter or cause to be heresy, but any such as heretofore have been . . . adjudged to be heresy by the authority of the canonical Scriptures, or by the first four General Councils, or any of them or by any other General Council wherein the same was declared heresy by the express and plain words of the said canonical Scriptures, or such as hereafter shall be ordered, judged or determined to be heresy by the High Court of Parliament of this realm, with the assent of the clergy in their Convocation'.

As we read the terms of the oath declaring the Queen to be supreme Governor and all the detailed clauses of the royal injunctions, or study the articles of episcopal visitations, we may well consider that the exactions of conformity were more than sufficient to hurt tender consciences. But the strain would have been infinitely greater if opinion had been made the test of church membership. The priesthood was certainly closed to those who accepted the doctrine of the Church of Rome, but only a comparative few found it impossible, especially under the rather lax administration of the Acts, to take the oath demanded of clergy and secular officials, and to acquiesce in the Elizabethan settlement. And, as for the Articles, subscription to which *was* required of the clergy in so far as they concerned the Christian faith and the doctrine of the Sacraments, their doctrine in matters of faith was acceptable to all Protestants.[1] Indeed, they have been subscribed by men of very various shades of opinion from that day to this. In matters of faith, the government did as little as it could to provoke the 'vice of damnable despair', which it deprecated in the sinner.[2]

After these general observations, we may confine ourselves to two aspects of English ecclesiastical history in this later stage of the Reformation: the administrative system of the Church, and the formation of the parties and interests which were either flatly opposed to it or did their best to alter it.

The Church of England is the most striking example in

[1] The recognition of his conformity required by the government of a clergyman in the diocese of Norwich in 1578 illustrates the attitude of the rather reluctant conformist. He willingly taught and professed the Articles to which Parliament required subscription. He admitted that the other Articles, touching ceremonies, discipline, and government, were not so imperfect as to justify refusal to attend church and to partake of the Sacraments. 'And further I do judge in my conscience and find by daily experience that the unnecessary teaching of such questions now in controversy in preaching or other public assemblies, to breed disquiet in the Church of God and to bring misliking of the State now present, are wisely to be foreseen, restrained and avoided.' The terms of the recognition were not in all points agreeable to Burghley, who made some very interesting alterations. Thus a note in his hand, afterwards cancelled, reads: 'that although some of the said ceremonies have been brought into the Church since the time of the Apostles, and might by public authority be altered or——yet none ought' (to refuse to come to the church, &c.). *Burghley Papers*, ii. 228–9.

[2] A phrase in the royal injunctions, where ministers are instructed to be ready with a store of comfortable words of Scripture, to save the sinner from the vice of damnable despair. It will be remembered that W. G. Ward differed from the other leaders of the Oxford Movement when he asserted that the Articles were incapable of construction in a 'Catholic' sense.

European history of the capacity of institutions to maintain an unbroken, almost complete, continuity in structure while undergoing a thorough change in spirit. Its courts and entire administrative system remained at work while it lost its connexion with the Western Church and was subjected to the daily interference of King, Council, royal ministers, commissioners, judges, municipal magistrates, and justices of the peace. Indeed they seemed to acquire new energy from a living principle which could not be defined either as ecclesiastical or secular, but was a curious compound, a sort of chemical resultant, of canonical traditions, a political reformation, and an enthusiasm caught from Strasbourg, Zürich, and Geneva. The Church continued to grant subsidies in Convocation though now they had formally to be sanctioned by a parliamentary statute, and so included in the secular revenue of the crown. It voted 'benevolences' or exceptional gifts to the crown, and these were collected under episcopal direction. Except in Mary's reign, tenths and first-fruits were paid by the clergy to the Crown as previously they had been paid to Rome, but the transaction was now under the control of a department in the Exchequer.[1] In spiritual affairs the Church exercised authority through the old system of provincial, episcopal, and archidiaconal courts and visitations, although now every excommunicated person could only be attached and imprisoned under a royal writ, and could invoke the decision of a secular court whether his offence fell within the competence of the ecclesiastical court.[2] The survival of ecclesiastical jurisdiction in civil and criminal cases which would now go to a secular court was very remarkable. The probate of wills and ecclesiastical control over matrimonial cases subjected the layman to canon law until

[1] Henry VIII had established a separate court, which was abolished by Mary when she refused to receive first-fruits. Elizabeth put first-fruits under the control of the Exchequer. The records of the department which dealt with them cover the period before the reign of William IV.

[2] 5 Eliz. c. 23 (1563).

Queen Victoria's time. Yet in the course of their general judicial and administrative work under parliamentary statute the ordinaries had often to suffer the concurrent jurisdiction of the Courts of Common Law.[1] Moreover, the most important and far-reaching jurisdiction in ecclesiastical cases was that of the mixed High Commission; and the archbishop's ordinary jurisdiction was subject to appeal to a mixed court of special delegates, whose various commissions came to be known as the 'High Court of Delegates in Ecclesiastical and Maritime Cases'.[2]

Two important matters required the creation of new machinery. The dissolution of the monasteries and chantries greatly increased the wealth at the disposal of the Crown and involved the Crown in responsibility for the dispossessed religious and clergy. Henry VIII established a separate Court of Augmentations to deal with the administration and disposal of his new property and to disburse the pensions. Some eleven years later he combined this court with that of the 'General Surveyors of the King's lands', a body which had grown out of an administration created by Henry VII. But this combined 'new Court of Augmentations' was abolished in Mary's reign when its business was transferred to the Exchequer. The business was extensive and onerous; it required a separate staff, which henceforward managed the Augmentation Office in the Exchequer. Several families of the new nobility owed their start in life to the opportunities provided by service in the Court or Office of Augmentations. As the pensioners died, one important set of duties gradually disappeared; but throughout Elizabeth's reign, the Office co-operated with the diocesan authorities in looking after the interests and morals of the men and women who

[1] e.g. when certain persons at the end of Elizabeth's reign began to teach systematically that infringement of the Sabbath was morally as bad as murder and adultery, both the archbishop and the Lord Chief Justice intervened.

[2] Act of 1534 (25 Hen. VIII, c. 19; see above, p. 51) and Act of 8 Eliz. c. 5 (1566).

had been thrown upon the world. In 1552, 1554, 1569, and 1575 general commissions of inquiry regarding the number of pensioners, and the difficulties in which they might be involved, were appointed. Some might have died, others received livings which made pensions unnecessary; some might have taken to evil ways, or married unhappily, or fallen into the hands of financial sharks.[1] If they had not succeeded in settling down, the dislike with which the secular clergy regarded them made their life all the more precarious and uncomfortable. As Mr. Baskerville observes: 'the parochial clergy looked upon them in the same light as the Anglican clergy of two generations ago looked upon Nonconformist ministers'.

An ex-monk could not take a benefice unless he could show his 'capacity', the faculty or dispensation which permitted him to be at large in the world. He was one of the numerous kinds of persons who, since the repudiation of Rome, had now to seek dispensations from the archbishop of Canterbury. This jurisdiction had been given to the archbishop by the lengthy Act of 1534 (25 Henry VIII, c. 21), which declared that the land was free from subjection to all human law not ordained within the realm, and claimed for Parliament the right to dispense from human law. The object was to continue in the archbishop the vast dispensing power previously exercised by the Pope. The canon law, so far as it was consistent with the law of the land or had not been repealed by statutory law, was operative in England. Under certain conditions dispensations from it had been freely granted; for example the faculty to take orders in spite of illegitimate birth, or to hold more than one benefice with cure of souls. The Papal power of dispensation was, as I have previously pointed out, essential to the smooth working of the complicated system of the Church. It was as essential after the breach

---

[1] A special Act was framed in the reign of Edward VI to protect them 'against crafty and deceitful buying of pensions'. For all this see Mr. Baskerville's article, quoted above (p. 33).

with Rome, hence the jurisdiction which, under careful safeguards, was passed on by the King in Parliament to the archbishop of Canterbury. The outcome was the Court of Faculties, whose officer, the Master of the Faculties, remained the possessor of a dignified, well paid, sinecure until his position was merged, in 1874, in that of the judge of the Court of Arches. In Elizabeth's reign the Court of Faculties had a good deal of business and responsibility, for it weighed heavily on the minds and consciences of the Protestant archbishops.[1]

One of the prevalent generalizations about the Elizabethan settlement is that episcopal government was lax or dispirited or inefficient. Sometimes we are told that the secular authorities shared the general dislike of ecclesiastical discipline, made light of excommunication, and undermined episcopal control by putting all the real power in the hands of the High Commission. Sometimes we are told that the incapacity of the bishops, or the essential feebleness of their administrative system, forced the government to take control, so far as it wished to take control itself. Or, again, the suggestion is made that the strength of the Presbyterian movement in Parliament and the Church, with its demand for a more elaborate, more articulated system of government on a local and democratic basis, was largely due to the worldliness and ineffectiveness of the bishops; while at the same time the bishops are condemned for their tyrannical interference with a healthy and natural development. Obviously these generalizations cannot all be true, even if they do not destroy each other. That between them they carry a good deal of truth is likely enough. No church can possess independent efficiency if it is penetrated at every part by political solicitude, and if its governing element is regarded as a branch of the civil service. As we have seen, efficiency in this sense was not desired. And no body of

[1] See Wilfred Hooper, 'The Court of Faculties' in the *English Historical Review* for October 1910 (xxv. 670–86).

bishops can escape the charge of despotism when it attempts to deal seriously with movements or reforms, as ably defended as were the various Puritanical and Presbyterian movements within the Elizabethan Church. The truth seems to be that we are not yet in a position to estimate, fairly or completely, the efficiency and range of ecclesiastical administration in the sixteenth century. The documents which reveal it have not yet been fully printed. Yet enough material is accessible to carry a very definite impression of normal and incessant activity, and to suggest that we should distinguish, more carefully than contemporary critics could be expected to distinguish, between the objections raised against the traditional diocesan system as such and the criticism of its effectiveness. Controversialists who on principle dislike the whole thing, with all its apparatus of temporal dignity, were not disposed to be just to those who had to maintain it, especially when their attempts to impose a different system involved them in pains and penalties. It should be remembered, moreover, that criticisms came from many sides and were the outcome of very different kinds of opinion. A secular-minded layman who chafed under the visitations of bishops and archdeacons might easily co-operate for a time with an anti-episcopal party whose rigid system of discipline would have roused him to fury if he had had to endure it. A defender of the existing order might well suggest reforms—for example, the substitution of a more localized pastoral administration by rural deans in place of the legalistic and often tiresome control by archdeacons[1]—which seem at first sight to bring him into line with the people whose influence he wished to destroy. Over against the controversial literature and the reports of judicial proceedings against the enemies of the ecclesiastical system,

[1] See, for example, the form of government drawn up by (John Becon), Chancellor of the Diocese of Norwich, in 1578 (*Burghley Papers*, ii. 195–8). Becon was a contentious person (see *Dict. Nat. Biog.*), but apparently a conscientious man with ideas of his own.

we must put the evidence of the episcopal registers, where
the details of provincial and diocesan rule can be studied
in the matter-of-fact happenings of every day. The episcopal records of that pious, hard-working, and excellent
man, Thomas Cooper, who graduated at Oxford in the
year of the Six Articles, and, as a convinced Protestant,
was made bishop of Lincoln in 1571, give a very different
picture of religious life. We see this good man, who was
never ashamed to confess that his father had been a needy
Oxford tailor, at the daily task, drawing up articles of
faith and practice, or a form of declaration for licensed
preachers, dealing with all kinds of disciplinary matters
as he sat as judge in his parlour at Buckden, supervising
the work of his archdeacons, arranging for the observance
of royal injunctions, and engaged in all the routine of his
office. Or, if we turn to the more important registers of
Archbishop Parker, we can study the working of the
medieval system of courts, visitations, administration of
vacant sees, trials, and excommunications.[1]

Clear thinking about the administration of the Elizabethan Church is not made easier by the tradition of persecution which attaches to it. After the first clean sweep of
the episcopal bench and the first visitations, there was little
persecution of any kind until the later years of Elizabeth's
reign; and the Catholic and Protestant martyrs of those
years were the willing or unwilling victims of the laws
which protected the Queen against treason or the Church
against schism. That they died for their faith they could
truly claim, and legal argument about the occasion of their
death may well appear to be callous and ironical quibbling
in the presence of their heroic suffering. Yet it was of great
moment for the future of toleration that in the eye of contemporary law their religion made them traitors, to use
Campion's phrase, and not heretics. Heresy, in the legal

---

[1] It is not necessary to describe the system in detail, and I would refer the
reader particularly to the late Bishop of Truro's introduction to Parker's
register, published by the Canterbury and York Society.

sense of the word, was rare; and rarely came before the old ecclesiastical courts. A wise convention was gradually accepted that the high commissioners were the appropriate judges in matters of heresy, and, as we have seen, the definition of heresy, embodied in the Act of Supremacy, carefully avoided the main causes of contemporary religious controversy. At the same time, the Elizabethan martyrs, and the more numerous sufferers, who endured imprisonment, suffered for their faith. They came to England, open-eyed, as missionaries of the Catholic Church, or they asserted the claims of conscience against the established order. In their pamphlets and sermons, and in their defence before the tribunals which dealt with them, they did not draw a line between their theology, their reading of past history, and their position as breakers of the law, nor were their judges careful to avoid the discussion of wider issues. If theological passion raged in every diocese, in episcopal parlours and from country pulpits, in quarter sessions, in Parliament and the Privy Council; if freedom of speech in the Court of High Commission was combined with the grim persuasiveness of the torture chamber, we cannot be surprised that in the eyes of posterity the reign of Elizabeth was a period of religious persecution. The exasperating difficulties which faced the bishops and the royal ministers, the constant striving after moderation and understanding, the acquiescence or indifference or absorption in other interests of common men and women, are all forgotten; although to the scholar the crusade of Jesuits, the recalcitrance of Puritan extremists and separatists, even the more extensive and more highly organized activities of the Presbyterian section in the Church, are but episodes worked into the background of the rich tapestry of Tudor history.

In the eyes of statesmen like Walsingham, for whom politics were, with much justification, a contest between Protestantism and Catholicism, light and darkness, Christ and Antichrist, these movements, often so secret, were dangerous and embarrassing enough. In times of intense crisis, they could become the occasion of general indignation and popular panic. But in the mind of the normal citizen in more normal times they stirred a more detached curiosity, not unlike the general attitude towards communism today. Doubtless the government knew its own business and how to deal with them.

The greatest danger which Elizabeth had to fear was the alliance against her of Spanish and Papal interests. King Philip did not usually find himself in accord with the Pope, but the possibility of a combined attack upon England could not be neglected. It was long in coming. The excommunication of Elizabeth by Pius V in 1570 was the result of rebellion in England, not of the willingness of Spain to enforce it. Its renewal by Gregory XIII in 1583 was due to the expectation of joint action by Scotland and France and the hope of Spanish support in a great crusade against England. But Philip was not to be ready for some years yet, and in the meanwhile Mary Queen of Scots was executed and Scotland lost to the Catholic cause. During all these years of anxiety, the English Catholics bore the brunt of each access of popular fear, of each precaution taken by the English government against surprise. And their plight was made worse by the energy of the Jesuit mission which at the same time confirmed their loyalty to the old faith. The reaction of English statesmen to the ever-changing moods of European politics can be traced in the history of anti-papal legislation for thirty years (1563–93) and of the severity or laxity with which it was administered.

Although the distinction between a supreme head and a supreme governor of the English Church was not grasped in Rome, and made little practical difference in the control of ecclesiastical affairs by the Crown, there seems to be no doubt that it made a real impression upon doubtful minds. The return to Papal authority in Mary's reign had brought home to English Catholics the impiety of a royal suprem-

acy which the ministers of Edward VI had exploited. The
protests of the bishops, headed by Heath, archbishop of
York, a man of moderate temper and intellectual ability,
had strengthened the reluctance of Elizabeth to resume
the title. Hence the royal injunctions which followed the
passing of the Acts of Supremacy and Uniformity warned
her people to pay no heed to the perverse and malicious
persons who deduced from the oath, recognizing Elizabeth to be the supreme governor, a challenge to the
'authority and power of ministry of divine offices in the
Church'. Many waverers were reassured, and although, as
we have seen, Protestant theologians made but small use in
the sixteenth century of the opportunity which this ad-
mission gave to them,[1] the hostility of English Catholics to
the new régime was moderated. Indeed, for some years
there was little evidence of the existence of a self-conscious
Catholic party in England. It was first shaken together in
the rebellion in the Catholic north in 1569, and was con-
solidated later by the efforts of the Jesuit mission. Yet even
after government severity and the thorough-going propa-
ganda of Parsons and other Jesuit leaders the English love
of compromise was not destroyed among the English
Catholics. Many resented the attempt to destroy their
allegiance to the Queen and to build up an English
organization under foreign control and not under a
native episcopate. They found evidence in history that
England had always taken an independent line in ecclesiastical affairs. They even groped after the possibility of a
national Catholic Church alongside the Established
Church and praised the mildness of the royal behaviour
towards them. They were inclined to be Elizabethan first
and Catholic afterwards, and established that equable

[1] A. O. Meyer, in his excellent work *England and the Catholic Church under
Queen Elizabeth* (English trans. 1916), p. 25, aptly quotes Selden's remark on
the difference between head of the Church and supreme governor. 'Con-
ceive it thus: There is in the Kingdom of England a college of physicians
the King is supreme governor of those, not the head of them, nor president
of the College, nor the best physician.'

tradition of staunch piety combined with insular moderation which was so offensive in the nineteenth century to
Cardinal Manning.

In 1559 Elizabeth published injunctions based upon
those of Edward VI, calling her people to obey the recent
statutes and submit to the jurisdiction of the ordinaries.
She also issued a series of commissions under letters
patent. One, which, with necessary changes in wording,
had as its model the letters of Edward and of Philip and
Mary, set up the High Commission, a body composed of
bishops, lords, theologians, and men learned in the law.
Reissued at various times during the reign, this commission gave permanence to what gradually became a powerful high court, independent of all other courts, competent
to supersede in important criminal matters every ecclesiastical jurisdiction and to concern itself with practically
the entire administration of the Church, as defined or
allowed by statute. It developed its own procedure, and
was the main instrument of discipline in the execution of
the legislation against popish recusants, Puritan recal-
citrants, and schismatics of all kinds. The other commissions issued in 1559 were temporary. England was
divided into six circuits, the northern province being one
of them. Small groups of divines, accompanied by a
preacher, and joined by gentry chosen from each area,
were sent round these circuits to impose the oath of
obedience, investigate the state of religion, and apply the
Acts. As they passed on from place to place, they left behind them local committees to carry on the work, to destroy altars, images, Catholic service books, and other
ornaments. Cases of discipline were generally referred to
the High Commission, but the visitors could deprive
priests who refused the oath, and commit them to cus-
tody. In testing the minds of the clergy, they required the
recantation of doctrines inconsistent with those prescribed
by public authority—'the authority of the pope, the
efficacy of good works as a means of justification, purga-

tory, the withholding of the cup from the laity, trans-substantiation, the reservation of the eucharist, prayers in an unknown tongue, pilgrimages, auricular confession, and the various minor observances which are included in the term sacramentals'.[1] No doubt the practice of the various groups varied, and in fact the government dealt sanely and moderately with the recusants, but the success of this thorough-going commission, dependent as it was upon local and lay support, and the ease with which the transition to the new order was made, show how little need Elizabeth had to fear resistance. Only some 300 clergy were deprived, by no means all for doctrinal reasons; they were allowed to settle down quietly or to leave the country; and as the Marian refugees from the Continent came trickling back with their set convictions and memories of foreign feuds, they found a Protestant Church awaiting them—a new bench of bishops, an English prayer-book and Bible, buildings despoiled of offence, a strong disciplinary authority, a laity (except in the north) of reforming sympathies, an acquiescent if unconvinced body of clergy. Indeed, as early as July 1559, the Spanish ambassador wrote that in six months the Queen 'has revived heresy and encouraged it everywhere to such an extent that it is recovering rapidly all the credit it had lost for years past'. No wonder that the Protestant extremists set to work with a will to shape the Church still nearer to their own pattern.

Yet, with their eyes on the Continent, and in their determination to allow no lead to a dogmatic clergy, the government, supported by a cautious archbishop, kept a moderate course. It is impossible to say how many Catholics there were in England at this time, waiting quietly for still another revolution. About 1583 the Catholic missionaries claimed that they had made 140,000 converts, a figure which, reduced to about 120,000, is now regarded as a fair estimate of the number, not of

[1] C. G. Bayne in *English Historical Review*, Oct. 1913, xxviii. 648.

converts from Protestantism, but of the Catholics who had the courage to confess their adherence to Rome and the Catholic faith. The number was small, and though it increased to nearer 200,000 before the end of the seventeenth century, it remained such, a mere fraction of the population of England.[1] The endurance of this steadfast element in English society has a significance clear enough in our day, though its ultimate results are still hidden in an uncertain future. Its significance in the history of Elizabeth's reign lies in the heroic obstinacy with which the Catholics endured the persecution in which the papal campaign against England involved them. They were the occasion, and the easiest victims, of one of the most dramatic crusades in history. Scores of ardent young men, trained by some of the best minds in Europe, inspired by leaders of genius, steeped in learned controversy, aglow with holy passion, dedicated to death, issued from the English colleges at Rheims and Rome on their mission to convert England. They had the most fantastic ideas of the prospects of success, but no amount of disillusionment could shake them. The story of the English movement on the Continent, of Cardinal Allen and Parsons and Campion, of the disputes between seculars and Jesuits, the sacrifice of innocent devotion to ecclesiastical expediency, the attempt to organize the Church in England, does not belong to this study of the English Reformation. Nor are we concerned with the statutes and administration which gradually made real and extended to laymen the penalty of treason which lay in wait in the Act of Supremacy. The story has often been told and must be read in full if it is to be truly judged. But the conflict reacted with great force upon the English Church. It sharpened Puritan feeling, gave form and character to English apologetics, and per-

---

[1] See the discussion in Meyer's book, pp. 59–73. Dr. Meyer gives much the best and clearest account of the whole subject of this section. For the transition from Mary's reign to the Elizabethan settlement see Bishop David Mathew, *The Celtic Peoples and Renaissance Europe* (London, 1933), especially the first three chapters.

suaded Englishmen that they were the allies of God in the war with His enemies.

The movements of opinion within the Church during Elizabeth's reign had more far-reaching results, more immediate and continuous influence than we could expect from the activities, however noble and disinterested, of the Catholics. The Puritan element in England was not composed of men who suffered or were proscribed. It could speak with authority and was entrenched in responsible positions, in Parliament and council chamber, in bishops' houses and cathedral chapters and benefices, in the Inns of Court and the universities. It ran through all shades of opinion, from docile submission to frank rebellion, and the line between permissible and illegal criticism was only gradually revealed. It must be regarded as an essential part of the spiritual life of the time, here glowing brightly with the sense of adventure, the passion for knowledge, the craving for beauty in all its forms, there earnest with schemes of social improvement, or drab with controversy, but always turbulent and vivacious. It was part of the Protestantism that exulted in the exploits of Drake and pointed triumphantly to the beneficial endowments of schools and colleges, hospitals and houses of charity. 'These charitable works' exclaimed Andrew Willet at the end of his catalogue of them, 'do glisten as pearls, and the workers thereof do shine as stars among us; their religious acts are as the pomegranates in Aaron's priestly garment, and themselves as the tinkling bells hanging thereon, do sound abroad the praises of the Gospel.'[1] Historians better acquainted than Willet was with the benefactions of the past and the social movements of his own time tell a different story, but the fact remains that religious thinkers were, in their way, sounding the depths of human nature, exploring knowledge, and casting about for the ways of

[1] The 'catalogue of good works' done in the sixty years following the accession of Elizabeth is included in the 1634 edition of Willet's *Synopsis Papismi*, pp. 1219–43.

improving society. They were of the time of Shakespeare and Bacon and the busy minds which framed the new Poor Law and brought new life to local government. The splendid work of Hooker sprang from the controversy with Presbyterian idealists, and the innumerable disputes about the governance of the Church were but part of the concern revealed in episcopal visitations, in archdeacons' courts, in the new organization of the parish, in preachings and pamphlets, for the social ordering of the Christian life. Beneath every expression of this activity, so often frustrated though it was by the new spirit of adventure and desire for gain, lay the belief in society as an organism, in which political and religious life worked in unison, as body with soul, under the guidance of a common head. The common law and the church law each had its appropriate place. It was the social duty of the ecclesiastical authorities to suppress usury and check greed and immorality, just as it was the social duty of the secular power to judge between man and man and to maintain order.[1] Episcopalian and Presbyterian quarrelled about the ways in which these duties were to be performed and laid the emphasis on different points, but they were agreed on the fundamental issue. And it should never be forgotten that the apostle of the congregational idea, Robert Browne, whose writings inspired the separatists, came back at last to the conviction that it was impossible to separate the secular from the spiritual power. Browne had no use for episcopal courts or Presbyterian synods or classes as agents of Christian discipline. He believed in the right and duty of each congregation to choose its own minister, and despairing of the magistrate, looked to minister and people to guide the Church in the way of God. But he did not think that this system was inconsistent with secular co-

---

[1] See especially R. H. Tawney, *Religion and the Rise of Capitalism* (1926), pp. 150–75. Some useful, though incoherent, information has been gathered together by Hans Leube in his short study: *Reformation und Humanismus in England* (Leipzig, 1930).

operation, or even with episcopal government. When he saw where pure separatism seemed to be tending, he fell back upon the magistrate. By 1588 he was ready to allow the magistrate control over every part of the life of the Church in its congregations. To deny the authority of bishops and magistrates is to overthrow all authority.

seeing there is no duty, law, deed, cause, question or plea which ought not to be spiritual, or is not determined by the divine and spiritual right, law, and word of God. And therefore the magistrates have power and a right of administration in all these things you named.

So, as solicitous as ever for the congregation, Browne in the study of this microcosm came to very much the same conclusion as his contemporary Hooker reached after ranging over the wide fields of human experience in thought and history. He had the same feeling about law, a much weaker regard for the organized Church, and a stronger belief in the magistrate.

It is from this general standpoint that the opposition to the episcopal system and the royal supremacy should be considered. The movement is usually regarded, and very naturally, as the source of later developments. Students of politics have fastened upon it as a significant factor in the history of constitutional government and of religious toleration. It emphasized the dilemma in the Elizabethan settlement, a dilemma of which toleration and parliamentary control were to be the working solutions. Ecclesiastical historians have deplored it or rejoiced in it as the case might be, because it destroyed the early dream of uniformity. These considerations did not enter the minds of the Presbyterians and Separatists; moreover, if we take too much account of them, we may do injustice to the settlement as a whole. The German scholar Troeltsch, for example, would seem to regard the English attempt to create a State Church as of little importance in comparison with the more fruitful experiments of its critics.

Most of the critics in fact were concerned, not to destroy the Anglican experiment but to develop it in their own way. They thought that the old bottles could hold new wine of still cruder quality. It is true that from an early date Englishmen can be found who deliberately rejected the argument from history in ecclesiastical matters, just as some were inspired by the new political learning to deny that the State owed any allegiance to its past or to the common law. But, on the whole, the appeal to history was more emphatic in England than it was elsewhere. The serious study of English history had begun, and the sense of continuity in English history was strengthened both by the patriotic spirit and by the whole course of the Reformation from 1534. Archbishop Parker, an ardent antiquarian, wrote a book about the Church of England which was really an historical treatise. When at the beginning of her reign Elizabeth stated that the English Church had been founded by Joseph of Arimathea she was simply repeating the lessons of the antiquaries. Englishmen with no interest in history were influenced by this faith in continuity; or at the very least were not prepared to approve of innovations which were not directed by the Crown, the traditional symbol of English unity. Thus Philip Stubbs, in the second part of his outspoken *Anatomie of Abuses*, while denouncing the evils of private patronage and pleading for a more independent and better-paid parish clergy, was emphatic in his support of episcopal government. The bishops, he said, should appoint to benefices on the nomination of the churches, patronage should be abolished, and vagrant ministers repressed, but there should be no drastic change in government. Stubbs did not believe in any divine right and had no theoretical objection to change; but his mind, so lively in the detection of evil, was guided by a regard for circumstances, by what he called common sense. 'Seeing it is the pleasure of the prince to bestow such dignity, authority, and honour upon them (the bishops), methink any sober christians should easily tolerate the same.'

Again, he agrees that it would be a good thing to have a 'seigniorie' or eldership in every congregation, but he regards it as impracticable and unwise. In apostolic times it was necessary, but now the Church can be governed by kings, princes, and governors. We must consider the state of the Church at this day: 'for in the Apostles' time, when seigniories were ordained, we read not of any shires, dioceses, or precincts, where bishops and ecclesiastical magistrates might exercise their authority and government as now they do'.

In short, though at one time, between 1570 and 1590, it would probably not have been difficult for the English Government to reconstruct the ecclesiastical system on presbyterian lines—for there was a great deal of sympathy with this tendency of Puritanism—there was no hope for any movement which involved disobedience and revolution. In some ways there was little difference between the very able teacher, Thomas Cartwright, the Cambridge scholar who led the Presbyterian movement, and people like Stubbs or Becon, whose proposals for a more human and intimate local government in the Church I have already noticed. The fabric or material of their criticism was similar to his. But whereas they, regarding themselves without any reservations as citizens of a Christian community, proposed changes which seemed expedient, and kept eclectic minds, Cartwright and his friends were inspired, just as Calvin and Hooker in their different ways were inspired, by a conception of what the Church should be. They had small patience with conscientious people who caused trouble about details like vestments, though of course they agreed with their views. They did not wish to press the issue between Church and State, although Archbishop Parker, and Whitgift in his turn, naturally saw a Scottish or Genevan system, if not a great revolutionary movement, as the outcome of their ideas. They believed in the co-operation of the magistrate and in his disciplinary functions as an independent, not as a subordinate, power. For years they 'tarried for the magistrate' and sought to have their way peaceably with the aid of Queen and Parliament. It is quite possible that, if they had been successful, the resulting system would have appeared a miserable compromise to Presbyterians elsewhere, just as the work of Cranmer and Ridley, whose position in the last years of Henry VIII's reign was very like that of Cartwright in the middle of Elizabeth's reign, did not satisfy the Continental reformers.

On the other hand, they differed from both Cranmer and Whitgift in imposing theoretical limitations upon obedience; and in the end they acted in accordance with their theory and tried to build up in secret assemblies and illicit 'classes' a system which they had hoped to see developed out of the local gatherings of clergy and the preachings tolerated in earlier years. The instincts of the Queen and bishops were justified, but that he had been forced to justify them was a far greater disappointment to Cartwright than it was to Elizabeth or Whitgift, for he was anything but a rebel.[1]

In this essay I have dealt with one main theme, the development out of the old order of an ecclesiastical system which was regarded as an integral part of the structure of society. So far as I could, I have subdued the discussion of theory to the task of explaining practice. With the details of theological and liturgical controversy I have not been concerned; nor have I dwelt upon the ever present element of human tragedy. The Reformation in England had its dramatic, even its grim moments, for religion in the sixteenth century could be a very grim business; but

[1] It is impossible to do justice in a brief account to the complicated story of the Presbyterian movement, and to what are known as the *classes* or local organizations, or to the relations of Cartwright with more unbalanced critics such as 'Martin Marprelate', or more thorough-going advocates of the independent church like Barrow and Greenwood, who would have been tolerated as little by Cartwright, if he had had his way, as they were by the government of Queen Elizabeth. See the valuable works of A. F. Scott Pearson, *Thomas Cartwright* (1925) and *Church and State; Political Aspects of Sixteenth-Century Puritanism* (1928).

to heighten the drama may be to obscure it. History can never afford to neglect the humdrum influence upon affairs, as they unroll themselves from day to day before an unknown and unregarded future, of the instinctive sanity of the common man, holding fast to his life in the security of an old, and established, commonwealth.